Making the Most of Your Meltdowns

Making the Most of Your of Your Meltdowns

BRENDA THOMAS

Every effort has been made to locate the authors or originators of the quotations and stories contained in this book. For additions, deletions, corrections, or clarifications in future editions of this text, please write Faith Library Publications.

16 15 14 13 12 11 10   07 06 05 04 03 02 01

Making the Most of Your Meltdowns
ISBN 13: 978-0-89276-983-4
ISBN 10: 0-89276-983-1

In the U.S. write:
Kenneth Hagin Ministries
P.O. Box 50126
Tulsa, OK 74150-0126
1-888-28-FAITH
www.rhema.org

In Canada write:
Kenneth Hagin Ministries
P.O. Box 335, Station D
Etobicoke (Toronto), Ontario
Canada, M9A 4X3
1-866-70-RHEMA
www.rhemacanada.org

Dedication

I want to dedicate this book to my precious family.

First of all, to my husband of over 30 years, Mark. Honey, thank you for always believing in me, encouraging me, and inspiring me! Your love has helped me grow into the person I am today.

To my two sons, John and James. I am proud of you and the men of God you have become. I count it a great honor and pleasure to be your mom.

To Lindy and Esther, my two daughters-in-law. You are both heaven sent. You are true gifts from God to your husbands and our family.

To Olivia, our little angel. Words cannot describe the joy and delight you have brought to our lives! Thanks for making me your "Grammy."

To all my church family at Heart of the Bay Christian Center. Your love and support has helped me soar to new heights!

And lastly, to my godly parents, John and Ruthie Edwards. Both of them have been in Heaven for many years, but their influence continues on in the lives of their children and grandchildren.

Table of Contents

Introduction

The message of this book was birthed from an accident that involved a batch of my famous chocolate chip cookies that I had baked for a church picnic. It soon turned into a humorous story through which the Lord revealed to me an invaluable truth.

It is my prayer that as you read this story and discover the truth from God's Word that surrounds it, there will be a smile on your face and joy in your heart.

The entire theme of this book is restoration. God is a Master at fixing any disaster. And He wants to restore every area of our lives and make them even better than before!

CHAPTER 1

The Meltdown

I am *not* a morning person! But on the particular Saturday morning when the meltdown occurred, I woke up bright and early because that was the day of our annual church picnic, an event that our church family looked forward to every year. It was also a day when I received lots of accolades and praise for my wonderful cooking abilities.

In order to continue a long-standing tradition and keep everyone from being disappointed, I had labored feverishly the night before on my famous chocolate chip cookies. It was such a beautiful batch! Each cookie was soft and chewy, huge in diameter, and they weighed in at about a quarter of a pound apiece. These babies were not low-calorie treats!

Just as I finished this tremendous cooking accomplishment, I spotted an ant leisurely crawling across my kitchen counter. Fear temporarily gripped my heart as I had a vision of him leading all of his relatives straight to my precious cookies. I also remembered that our youngest son, James, would be home soon. He might have friends with him who would devour my tempting treasures if they were anywhere in sight.

I had grown up on a farm in rural Oklahoma, and my mother had taught her daughters how to combat the elements of country living, such as ants in the pantry. I could hear her voice ringing in my ears—"Put your freshly baked sweets in the oven. The ants won't go in there." What a great idea! Those cookies would be safe from all creatures, both four-legged and two-legged, if I put them in the oven. So I sealed them securely in the biggest Tupperware® containers I owned, placed them in the oven, and proceeded to go to bed.

The next morning I woke up bright and early and headed to my kitchen to complete my cooking feat for the picnic. We always asked our church family to bring two dishes to share. Since I am the "perfect" pastor's wife, of course I would bring at least three. In addition to my cookies, this year I had elected to bring a ham and baked beans, both of which need to be baked in the oven. As mentioned before, I am *not* a morning person, so please keep in mind that I was still half asleep when the following events occurred.

All good cooks know that you always preheat the oven before baking anything. So I set the oven on 350 degrees, turned my back, and started opening all of those cans of beans. My kitchen quickly filled with a disgusting scent. *What is that awful smell?* I wondered. *Somebody must be burning plastic or something else in their backyard. Don't they know that's illegal in California?* I was completely clueless about the fact that my precious cookies were at that very moment being offered up as a burnt sacrifice in those large plastic Tupperware containers.

By this time, my husband, Mark, had come downstairs. He commented on the smell, to which I replied, "I know. It *is* awful, isn't it? Somebody is burning something." He opened the back door, sat down on the couch in our family room, and made a phone call. About that time, I finally turned around and faced my stove, only to witness flames leaping around in my oven. Oh, no! My cookies were on fire. Duh!

It was too late to save that beautiful batch of cookies. The high levels of sugar and butter in the cookies, combined with the plastic of the Tupperware containers, had created an extremely combustible situation.

I screamed, "Fire!" and Mark, my knight in shining armor, immediately told the friend he was talking to that he had to hang up because I was "burning down the kitchen or something." I think he was in disbelief as we both just stood there and watched the flames slowly die down.

At least I had enough presence of mind not to open the oven door, or this story could have been much worse. All I could think about was the destruction of my beautiful cookies. But then Mark pointed out that there was a bigger issue involved—the melted plastic and hardened sugar that coated the oven coils.

"Do you think the oven is ruined?" he asked cautiously.

As the seriousness of the situation began to sink in on me, I suddenly had a fit of carnality. Out of my mouth came the words, "I hate the dumb church picnic! I have always hated it. I don't like playing sports and those stupid games, and I don't enjoy watching everybody else play them. This is it! *I am not going to the dumb picnic!*" Basically, I was saying the picnic had caused this disaster. That makes a lot of sense, doesn't it?

At that moment, Mark did what any smart husband would have done. He left! As he escaped out the door, he mumbled something about going to the picnic and needing to get some pies or something to take with him.

Shortly after he left, the phone rang. It was our friend, Tony Cooke. He was the one Mark had been talking to when this whole episode had occurred. He started the conversation by saying, "Brenda, is everything all right? How is your kitchen?"

As I proceeded to give him the details of what I had done, he tried to sound compassionate. But I could tell from the fluctuation in his voice that he was about to burst out laughing. Finally I gave him permission to laugh, which helped me see the humor in the situation.

Tony is very creative and sees a sermon in everything. He quickly told me what a great illustrated sermon this story would make and that I should call it, "Making the Most of Your Meltdowns." That's how I got the title of this book. Thanks, Tony!

As for the rest of the story, I quickly repented, got myself together, and went to the "wonderful" church picnic. Mark and I agreed not to talk about why there were no cookies this year. We had been at the picnic a total of about five minutes when all the questions began. My husband, not willing to expose his wife's ignorance, wasn't saying a word. Finally, I said, "Okay, this is what happened to my cookies."

News of the meltdown quickly spread throughout the park. I was surprised at how happy some of the ladies seemed to be that their "perfect" pastor's wife had done something so stupid. We seemed to be forming a new bond as they related to me their own cooking horror stories.

One precious lady, who I lovingly call Mother Pauline, had some great advice for me. She was 91 years young at that time, and I'm sure she had heard many outrageous tales of things people had done in their kitchens. She boldly said, "Honey, don't worry about ruining your oven. Call your homeowner's insurance company. I'll bet they will take care of it." Out of respect, I didn't ask her how she knew that. But I couldn't wait to make that call.

When we got home, I gathered my insurance information and dialed the claims number. Since it was late Saturday afternoon, I fully expected to get a recording. But I was shocked when I connected with a live person. As the agent questioned me about the nature of my call, I began to relate the incident by saying, "Do we have a clause in our policy for stupidity?"

Much to my delight, she responded with, "Sure you do. Just tell me your story." I went through the whole scenario, sparing no details. She patiently listened and then stated, "I will have a claims adjuster call you on Monday, but it sounds to me like you are getting a new stove."

A thrill went through my spirit as I realized what was happening. God's favor was working on my behalf, and He was teaching me about His love and mercy, which *always* supersedes our mistakes. A message was being birthed in my heart that would not only bless my life but also help others receive the goodness of our God. He is so much bigger than our shortcomings and failures!

'Where Are the Melted Cookies?'

Early Monday morning the phone rang, and it was a cheerful insurance agent. I woke up quickly for this call, even though as I said before, I'm *not* a morning person. He had read the report filed on Saturday but wanted me to repeat the incident to him. His only question was, "Where are the melted cookies now? Did you attempt to clean your oven?"

I told him that the cookies were pretty much *cemented* to the bottom of the oven. I hadn't attempted to remove them, since it would be almost impossible without some kind of heavy equipment.

My response seemed to be what he was looking for, and I was once again thrilled when I heard him say that it sounded like I was getting a new stove. All he wanted me to do was price some comparable stoves and have the information ready for him when he came to look at my stove on Tuesday. With much excitement, I set out to find my dream range.

Did I mention that my old stove was 18 years old? It was the one that had been installed when the house was first built. We had recently refaced our kitchen cabinets and installed a new dishwasher. But when I mentioned that I would like to replace the stove, my wonderful husband strongly suggested that we wait until another time.

Warning: do not try to recreate this scenario at home! I don't want to be blamed for some new insurance scam that involves breaking your appliances on purpose so your homeowner's insurance will be forced to replace them. This was truly an accident, and that is why the story ended the way it did.

It didn't take long to locate the stove I wanted. I found one at a nearby store, and all I needed to do was wait for Tuesday's appointment. The agent was prompt in arriving, and as soon as he asked to see my stove, I escorted him into the kitchen. All he did was open the oven door and quickly say, "Yep, you are getting a new stove."

Since this was my first time to destroy an appliance, I didn't know what the replacement procedure would be. Would they mail me a check? Would I have to fill out an enormous amount of paperwork? Would there be a lot of red tape?

My questions were suddenly answered when the adjuster asked to see the prices of the stoves I had picked out the day before. All he said was, "Those are reasonable quotes," and then he pulled out his calculator. You can imagine my surprise when he also took out a checkbook and stated that he was going to compensate me today for the price of a new stove, minus the $250 deductible.

In my stunned state, all I could manage to say was, "Of course, that's right. We *do* have a $250 deductible on our policy." He graciously handed me the check, I thanked him, and we said our goodbyes. After he left, I was still in disbelief that this had all taken place so rapidly. Was this normal, or had I just encountered some kind of divine intervention?

The Lord ministered to my heart in such a precious way, assuring me that He *had* gotten involved in this matter. He wanted me to understand how much He loves me and never question His ability to turn every situation around for good. He is truly the Master at fixing every disaster!

An overwhelming sense of peace and thanksgiving rested on me as I set out to purchase my new stove. The favor of the Lord was encompassing me like a shield (Ps. 5:12). It was indeed one of the most enjoyable shopping adventures I had ever had. My stove was delivered in record-breaking time, and my kitchen was open for business again by Friday.

That was when I started working on a message to be delivered to our congregation the following Sunday night. Of course, the title was "Making the Most of Your Meltdowns." I included all the details of this story, as well as sharing about God's restoring power. The message of this book started with that sermon, but God kept adding to it!

It's important to give an account here of what occurred on the night I ministered this sermon to our church, because it continues to illustrate the goodness of our God. Toward the end of the message, I mentioned the fact that our insurance company paid for everything except the $250 deductible. At the close of the service, a dear lady came up to me with tears in her eyes, handed me an envelope, and said, "The Lord spoke to my heart while you were sharing tonight and told me to tell you that He doesn't want you to pay for any of this mistake." Inside the envelope was a check for $250.

You can imagine how overwhelmed I felt. I thought, *God You are too much! Oh, how You love me!* Most of the time we have no trouble telling our Father God how much we love Him. But we sometimes have difficulty comprehending how much He loves us and wants to manifest His goodness in our lives.

I am in no way saying that melting cookies in my oven can in any fashion compare to the real-life tragedies that so many have faced. However, I trust the lessons the Lord has taught me through this experience can serve as encouragement to others that God will help us overcome any mistake or disaster. As you read these next few chapters, may the reality of God's goodness and mercy sink deep into your soul.

CHAPTER 2

Can You Relate?

There is not a person alive who hasn't made more than one mistake. We've all said and done things that we have later regretted. I know sometimes I've said something and then I wanted to go back and say, "Oh, let's rewind that tape. I didn't really mean that." We'd all like to be able to go back in time and say, "Hey, let's wipe that out of our memories."

When I shared my meltdown story with our congregation and also at several women's conferences, I heard all sorts of culinary disaster stories, not to mention other types of blunders and bloopers. Let me clarify something here. It is not only women who have "blond moments," "lapses of good sense," or even "hormone-from-hell days." Men do dumb things too!

My husband, Mark, as wonderful as he is, isn't exempt from messing up, in spite of the scripture the Lord gave me regarding him when we were dating. It was Psalm 37:37 (KJV)—*"Mark the perfect man. . . ."* My husband of over 30 years is an awesome man of God, a great pastor, and an eloquent orator and preacher of the Word. But he has committed some really great pulpit bloopers over the years.

With his permission, I'll share just one. This happened to involve performing a wedding ceremony. Mark and I were fairly new pastors in the San Francisco Bay Area. This was almost 25 years ago, and all sorts of people were getting born again and attending our church services. We were delighted with what God was doing, and we were receiving people from all walks of life and different backgrounds with open arms into our new and thriving congregation.

One such convert was a musician from a Christian rock band who had long, jet-black hair. When he attended our church services, he pulled his flowing locks back into a ponytail, so we hadn't really gotten the full impact of his hairdo. Then the day came when he asked us to perform his wedding ceremony, which we happily agreed to do. Mark and I were going to officiate at the marriage together. So when we arrived at the location of the big event, we were directed to a back room where the groom was anxiously awaiting the beginning of the ceremony.

I must admit we were both taken a little by surprise when we saw him. It appeared he had recently gotten a perm, and he had *really big hair*! But even this encounter couldn't have prepared us for what we witnessed when we stepped out onto the platform. One by one, the groomsmen (who were also members of the band) marched down the aisle. Each one's hair seemed to be bigger and longer than the one before them. It was quite a sight! The guys in the wedding had *more* and *bigger* hair than the girls. We had never seen a wedding party like this one.

My husband, being the professional that he is, began the ceremony by boldly blurting out his opening line—"Shall we bow our *hair* for prayer." I am usually very quick to catch all of Mark's bloopers so I can kindly point them out to him. But I didn't even notice he had said anything wrong. Given the situation, I guess his comment seemed accurate to me. The funny thing is that no one else laughed either, and it wasn't until some time later that we discovered the blunder.

Over the years, this incident has provided much joy and laughter for us. Sometimes, I think God allows our human side to take over just to get us to lighten up, stop taking ourselves so seriously, and stop over-spiritualizing our mistakes.

We're all looking for someone else to blame. Who caused this? Was it the devil? Was it God? In reality, most of the time we just need to look in the mirror and admit, "I blew it. I failed. I really messed up." The right response is to recognize our part in the situation, admit our wrongdoing, and tell those we may have hurt or offended that we are sorry. Then we need to repent before God, receive His forgiveness, forgive ourselves, and move on.

Have you ever thought about the fact that even though the Bible tells us in Genesis 1:26 that God created man in His likeness and image, man is not infallible? We are human beings, and human beings are going to have moments of imperfection. We are going to:

- Forget the cookies are in the oven
- Leave the coffee pot on all day
- Forget to turn the curling iron off
- Leave the dog locked outside
- Forget to pick the kids up from soccer practice

Obviously, the list could go on and on. What do we do on days like that? Sit down and have a "pity party"? "Why God, why? Why is this happening to me? I am such a victim of this unseen plot to destroy me."

I am not minimizing the fact that, as believers, we *do* have an enemy called the devil. He *does* devise plots and plans to try and trip us up and lead us into temptation. But God has given man something very powerful called the human will. With the Lord's help, we can make choices that will keep us on the path to enjoying the good life He's promised us in His Word. And we can also learn to continually let go of what has happened in the past. When we have missed it, we must use our will and make a conscious decision to act on what the Word of God tells us to do.

One device the enemy uses to paralyze people and keep them from moving forward in life is condemnation. Romans 8:1 says, *"There is therefore now no condemnation to those who are in Christ Jesus, who do not walk according to the flesh, but according to the Spirit."*

One definition of *condemn* is "to declare unfit for use." That alone should assure us that God is not into condemnation. He doesn't create any junk and He has no unusable members in His family. There is no one who is unfit for the Kingdom of God.

The devil is the one who feeds people those kinds of lies and tries to keep them in bondage because of some mistake from their past. Fear of failure is at the root of that kind of bondage. Satan whispers, "You failed once, so don't step out again. You will only mess up!" Does that sound like our loving Father Whose mercy endures forever? I don't think so. He is the God of the second, third, and fourth chance—or as many chances you need!

Living on God's Timetable

Another trick of the enemy is to condemn us about the time we wasted before we knew the Lord or even after we were born again but weren't fully walking with Him. The Lord spoke to a good friend of mine as she was ministering one time and told her that He wanted her to minister to all of those who were living in regret.

He said, "Many of My people are spending too much time in their prayer closets, crying over wasted years and mistakes they have made. Many of My people are boo-hooing over, 'God, I didn't get saved until later in life and I made a mess of things before I knew You. Oh Lord, I wasted all of those years.'"

God is not so concerned about those 20, 30, or even 40 years that we weren't serving Him. He's not uptight about it. And He wants us to get over it! He wants us to let it go and make the next 40 years the best we possibly can.

In other words, God isn't hung up on your past. He doesn't see it as a major bummer if you got saved at age 40. He doesn't say, "Oh boy, that's too bad. There's no time left for Me to use them." No, those 40 years are only a brief span of time on God's timetable. As far as He is concerned, there is still plenty of time. You are never too young or too old to be effective in doing the work of the Lord.

No matter what your age, refuse to live in the past. Refuse to live in regret. Put the past behind you, look toward the future, and be useful in the Kingdom of God. He wants to use every single one of us! He is so merciful. He is so full of loving-kindness that He is not holding anything that you've ever done over your head. He doesn't have a stamp that says "unusable." He doesn't write that on anybody's forehead. Every one of us is valuable and precious to Him.

I like what the Bible says in verse 9 of Second Peter chapter 3. *"The Lord is not slack concerning His promise, as some count slackness, but is longsuffering toward us, not willing that any should perish but that all should come to repentance."* Our Father is longsuffering. He is patient. He's expecting everyone to repent. That's His target. He's going after every single one.

This verse says that He's not slack concerning His promises. I dare say that you may have been born again because someone who knew you—a grandma, great-grandma, grandpa, uncle, or aunt—prayed for you and stood on the Word of God, believing for you to be saved. And God honored their prayers and faith. He is faithful to a thousand generations.

Even if there was not a godly, praying person in your family, God was still using someone to pray that your heart would be softened and you would turn to Him. Because of those prayers, an anointed laborer was sent across your path. Thanks be to God!

Your mistakes are not greater than His Grace. You are valuable and precious to Him, and He has an awesome plan in store for you!

CHAPTER 3

Get Over It!

Perhaps you are reading this book and you have not yet asked Jesus into your heart. I want to assure you of God's love for you. Your past sin and failures do not matter to Him, nor will they keep His saving power from giving you a brand-new life. What you did yesterday does not matter. What you said today does not matter. No sin is so great that the mercy of our Lord Jesus Christ cannot wipe it clean.

God is reaching out in love to draw you to Himself. No matter where you have been or what you have done, the shed blood of His precious Son will cover it all. The revelation of this truth is not only necessary for an unbeliever to be saved, but it is also a vital truth to help those of us who are already born again live free from condemnation and learn to walk in victory.

You see, the enemy loves to remind us of our past mistakes and failures, but that is not our Heavenly Father's nature. He is not holding our trespasses against us. As a matter of fact, He doesn't even want to remember them! Psalm 103:12 says, *"As far as the east is from the west, So far has He removed our transgressions from us."* And Isaiah 43:25 tells us, *"I, even I, am He who blots out your transgressions for My own sake; And I will not remember your sins."*

17

He said, "For My own sake," didn't He? God doesn't want to remember all of that junk! Can you imagine Him trying to remember all the things that a person has ever done wrong? No! Thank God for the precious blood of the Lamb that washes us white as snow!

Micah 7:19 in *The Amplified Bible* says, *"He will again have compassion on us; He will subdue and tread underfoot our iniquities. You will cast all our sins into the depths of the sea."* God takes our sins and casts all of them into the sea of forgetfulness. And someone once added that He puts up a sign that says, "No fishing!" The sins are gone forever. If He is not willing to bring up those things, then you shouldn't be either. You don't need to repent over and over again for something you did 20 years ago. God has already forgotten it.

Besides, we need to have faith in the blood of the Lamb. The blood has the power to save. The blood also has the power to cleanse us. First John 1:9 says, *"If we confess our sins, He is faithful and just to forgive us our sins and to cleanse us from all unrighteousness."*

When we miss it, we should see ourselves getting into God's washing machine, filled with the precious blood of the Lamb. The sinless, spotless blood of Jesus contains the greatest cleansing agent there is. It removes every spot, wrinkle, or stain! It puts them all under the blood.

When you've asked God for His forgiveness, I encourage you to forgive yourself and move on. And you have to do the same with other people. I've heard people say things like, "Well, they said they were sorry, and since I am a Christian I will have to forgive them. But I will never forget what they said or did to me."

If we are not willing to let go of what other people have done to us, we're not going to walk in God's best. We're going to hinder the power of God from flowing into our bodies, our finances, and every other area of our lives. It's a twofold application. We have to forgive *and* we have to forget. Unforgiveness toward ourselves and others will only hold *us* in bondage. And it will keep us from moving into God's glorious plan for our lives.

A Man With a Colorful Past

There is a wonderful example in the Bible of a man of God who had a colorful past. Have you ever heard of the Apostle Paul? Before he became Paul, his name was Saul, and his occupation was "persecutor of the Church." I believe the Holy Spirit gave him the beautiful revelation found in Philippians chapter 3 because of the things from his past that he had to forgive himself for and forget:

PHILIPPIANS 3:10-11 (Amplified)

10 [For my determined purpose is] that I may know Him [that I may progressively become more deeply and intimately acquainted with Him, perceiving and recognizing and understanding the wonders of His Person more strongly and more clearly], and that I may in that same way come to know the power outflowing from His resurrection [which it exerts over believers], and that I may so share His sufferings as to be continually transformed [in spirit into His likeness even] to His death, [in the hope]

11 That if possible I may attain to the [spiritual and moral] resurrection [that lifts me] out from among the dead [even while in the body].

The Apostle Paul experienced a dramatic conversion, a supernatural encounter with the Lord on the road to Damascus. He knew the power of God was at work in him, yet he wrote in this passage that it was his determined purpose to become more deeply and intimately acquainted with the Lord Jesus. We should never reach a place in our Christian walk where we cease to discover and stand in awe of the wonders of His Person. Let us continue to read from this passage:

PHILIPPIANS 3:12–14 (Amplified)

12 Not that I have now attained [this ideal], or have already been made perfect, but I press on to lay hold of (grasp) and make my own, that for which Christ Jesus (the Messiah) has laid hold of me and made me His own.

13 I do not consider, brethren, that I have captured and made it my own [yet]; but one thing I do [it is my one aspiration]: forgetting what lies behind and straining forward to what lies ahead,

14 I press on toward the goal to win the [supreme and heavenly] prize to which God in Christ Jesus is calling us upward.

In these verses, the Apostle Paul set out some powerful truths about letting go of the past. His main point is that we are not to dwell there. Instead, we must realize our past is under the blood, and we must forget it!

Just think about what an awesome man of God Paul turned out to be, when just a few years earlier he had been tormenting the Church. And by tormenting, I don't mean that he was just making fun of or joking about Christians. No, he was having them thrown into prison and stoned to death. He was doing all sorts of terrible things to the Church of the Living God.

Can you imagine the guilt he had to deal with after he was born again? Perhaps he went to a Bible study, and Sister Sue said to him, "Apostle Paul, I forgive you for having my husband killed." Think about it.

Or maybe he walked over to another woman and she told him, "Paul, I forgive you for having my son imprisoned because we were Christians."

These are the real kinds of things that he did to real people. And perhaps he did meet some of their relatives. After all, he ministered in the same churches that he had tormented and the same places where he had people arrested. Can you imagine the regret and horror he must have felt because of the things he had done to his fellow believers?

That's why I believe he wrote this chapter. He said, "I choose to forget the past. I choose to forget those things which lie behind me. That man called Saul, who was a persecutor of the Church, died on the road to Damascus. He's no longer here. I'm a brand-new creature in Christ Jesus."

Paul had to get the revelation of pressing forward. He had to let go of his past, so that he could reach for and press toward the future. He wrote an interesting passage regarding his past to Timothy:

1 TIMOTHY 1:12–14

12 And I thank Christ Jesus our Lord who has enabled me, because He counted me faithful, putting me into the ministry,

13 although I was formerly a blasphemer, a persecutor, and an insolent man; but I obtained mercy because I did it ignorantly in unbelief.

14 And the grace of our Lord was exceedingly abundant, with faith and love which are in Christ Jesus.

Before Paul had an experience with the Lord on the road to Damascus, he was one bad dude. But grace came upon him. God anointed him for his race. He changed him from Saul to Paul and set him in the ministry. God enabled Paul to do what he did because all the things he had done in the past were done ignorantly. He didn't know who he was persecuting. He didn't know that Jesus was the real Christ.

Have you ever done something in ignorance? Have you ever had to say, "I plead ignorance? I made a dumb mistake. I just flat didn't know any better." Has anybody besides me ever done that? We can all attest to it.

Ignorance is not bliss, but it is forgivable. Often, we do things we later regret, either due to immaturity, lack of sound judgment, or just poor insight. Whatever the reason, we cannot go back and relive the past or change something that's caused us remorse. It isn't possible to unscramble eggs. But once we recognize our mistakes, we can make a quality decision to change and not allow history to repeat itself.

Once the Apostle Paul received the revelation of Who Jesus really was, he did not hesitate to believe in Him and acknowledge Him as his Lord and Savior. He also had to make a quality decision not to live in the past, but to accept that Christ had made him a brand-new person and had a plan and purpose for his future. Why is that so important? Because we can't hold on to things from the past and at the same time try to reach toward the future.

The Spirit of God had given Paul the revelation that he had to leave the past behind and grasp with all of his heart what lay ahead of him. He had to grasp with purpose why God's hand was upon him. He settled it on the inside—in his spirit. He was saying, in essence, "God's hand is upon me for good, I'm not an unworthy worm. I'm not the same man that I used to be. Now I'm a child of the Living God. I'm going to lay hold of all that God wants me to be."

If Paul had not been able to leave the past behind, he would not have been able to walk out God's plan for his life and become what he was created to be. And neither will you. You have to let the past go. You can't reach toward the future if you're holding on to the past. Your attitude should be the same as a slogan on a T-shirt I bought for our boys when they were small. It had all of these animals on it that were dressed in colorful clothes and wearing sunglasses. The slogan said, "My future is so bright, I have to wear shades!"

God Is Calling You Upward

I like what it says in verse 14 of Philippians chapter 3: "*I press on toward the goal*" (Amplified). Paul had a goal. He had a purpose—to win the supreme and heavenly prize to which God in Christ Jesus is calling us . . . *downward*? Is that what it says? Does God call us *downward*? Does God drag us through the mud, crud, muck, and mire to teach us something? No! God always calls us *upward*.

The Bible says in Psalm 3:3, "*But You, O Lord, are a shield for me, My glory and the One who lifts up my head.*" I love these definitions of the word *lift*:

1. To raise

2. To elevate

3. The aerodynamic force acting on an aircraft that is exerted in an upward direction, opposing the pull of gravity

As believers, we have a force or power from God available to us that defies all natural laws. It is greater than all the tactics, strategies, and lies of the enemy. You see, the devil tries to pull us *down* because he is headed down into the pit. But God always pulls us *up*. He lifts us up to our rightful place in Him.

If thoughts are coming against you that pound you on the head and make you start looking down and feeling so oppressed that you can't even raise your head, just know that God is not trying to teach you a lesson through those thoughts. He's not trying to make you feel guilty. He never does that.

God deals with us lovingly. He will correct us, but He never makes us feel unworthy in the process. It's not His nature. God lifts us upward, always reaching down and pulling us up to His level.

Unfortunately, there are too many people—even Christians—who spend their vacation time in a place called the "City of Regret." Have you ever visited there? I can assure you that the Holy Spirit wasn't the booking agent for that trip. And if you're spending some time there right now, it's time to check out. I read an account of a trip to the City of Regret that I'd like to share with you.

"Leaving the City of Regret"

I had not really planned on taking a trip this time of year, and yet I found myself packing rather hurriedly. This trip was going to be unpleasant, and I knew in advance that no real good would come of it. I'm talking about my annual "Guilt Trip."

I got tickets to fly there on *Wish I Had* airlines. It was an extremely short flight.

I got my baggage, which I could not check. I chose to carry it myself all the way. It was weighted down with a thousand memories of what might have been.

No one greeted me as I entered the terminal to the Regret City International Airport. I say international because people from all over the world come to this dismal town.

As I checked into the Last Resort Hotel, I noticed that they would be hosting the year's most important event, the Annual Pity Party. I wasn't going to miss that great social occasion. Many of the town's leading citizens would be there.

First, there would be the *Done* family—you know, Should Have, Would Have, and Could Have.

Then came the *I Had* family. You probably know ol' Wish and his clan.

Of course, the *Opportunities* would be present—Missed and Lost.

The biggest family would be the *Yesterdays*. There are far too many of them to count, but each one would have a very sad story to share.

Then *Shattered Dreams* would surely make an appearance.

And *It's Their Fault* would regale us with stories (excuses) about how things had failed in his life, and each story would be loudly applauded by *Don't Blame Me* and *I Couldn't Help It*.

Well, to make a long story short, I went to this depressing party knowing that there would be no real benefit in doing so. And, as usual, I became very depressed.

But as I thought about all of the stories of failures brought back from the past, it occurred to me that all of this trip and subsequent "pity party" could be cancelled by ME!

I started to truly realize that I did not have to be there. I didn't have to be depressed. One thing kept going through my mind—I can't change yesterday, but I do have the power to make today a wonderful day.

—by Larry Harp from MountainWings.com

If you have found yourself getting on a flight to the "City of Regret," just recognize that it's a trip you've booked all by yourself, and you can cancel it at any time without penalty or fee. But you're the only one who can.

There's a lot of truth in that story, and none of us wants to spend time in the "City of Regret." I am not minimizing the difficulties you may have encountered and the hard places you may have been in. But through God's grace, you can get over it. You can recover and still have a fruitful life.

The problems that all of us face can impact us in one of two ways. We'll either experience a breakdown or a break-through. No breakdowns, please! Do you want to have a breakthrough? God can turn your messes around!

The devil may have knocked you down but he hasn't knocked you out. It's not over until it's over. I like something that a good minister friend of mine once said—"Don't let a setback make you sit back. Instead, prepare for a comeback." You're coming back stronger than ever before!

If the devil has attacked you in your physical body and you had to have surgery, don't be bothered about it. Just rise up and come back stronger. Get healthier and go out and lay hands on the sick and give the devil a big, black eye.

If your kids have been rebellious, don't go to the "City of Regret" and live in self-pity. Just go out and find some teenagers and lead them to the Lord. Rise up. Retaliate!

Jesus did exactly that after the cruel beheading of his cousin John the Baptist. (See Matthew chapter 14.) Herod's stepdaughter asked for John's head on a platter after she had performed a provocative dance for her stepfather and his guests. How disgusting is that?

Jesus knew it was the devil who had inspired the girl and her mother, Herodias, to make that request. The Lord knew who the real source of this incident was. It wasn't flesh and blood, even though the people involved had yielded to demonic forces and ungodly thoughts. The real enemy behind this scheme was Satan himself.

Jesus retaliated by doing harm to the devil's kingdom. He went out and healed the sick, cast out devils, and raised the dead. I love it! It was as if He was saying, "Take that, Mr. Devil. You may have killed My cousin, but I am going to set multitudes of your captives free!"

That should be our attitude also. We should rise up and declare to the devil that he has messed with the wrong person and he is going to pay, big time! As believers, we should have some fight in us—not fighting each other, but fighting the good fight of faith.

Even if you have lost some battles, you won't lose the war if you will rise up, get over it, and walk in your God-given authority!

CHAPTER 4

Hey, God! Where Were You?

James 1:2 says, *"My brethren, count it all joy when you fall into various trials."* Have you ever been trucking down the road of life and all is going well, when out of nowhere you seem to fall into this bottomless pit of tests and trials? You cry out to God, you search your heart, but you don't discover any huge, unconfessed sin that could have caused this calamity. You don't receive any deep revelation about a gigantic door you left open to the devil.

There are times when unexplainable attacks do come, just by virtue of the fact that we live in an imperfect world and have to deal with an enemy who wants to steal God's Word and the joy of the Lord out of our hearts. Let me give you a few examples of the attacks I'm talking about here:

1.   The marriage you thought was secure ends in divorce because of an unfaithful mate.

2.   Your sweet teenage daughter becomes pregnant.

3.   The company where you have worked for 20 years closes, causing enormous financial pressure.

4.   Grief tries to overtake you after the sudden and untimely death of a loved one.

The list could go on and on. Bad things do happen to good people! When this occurs, we all have a choice to make. We can either become bitter or get better. I personally have had to make this choice on numerous occasions. I'd like to share one of those with you.

On September 11, 1975, which happened to be my 21st birthday, my mother had surgery to remove a mass from her colon. The surgery revealed something none of us were prepared for. We were told that she had colon cancer, which had already spread to her liver. The prognosis was very grim. My precious mother elected not to do any treatment and was sent home to await the outcome of this devilish disease.

As I mentioned earlier, I grew up on a farm in rural Oklahoma. Life on a farm is both demanding and hectic, and the livestock and crops require constant attention. To add even more stress to the situation, my dad had begun working a part-time job to help supplement the family income because the farming industry was not doing well at the time. We all knew it would be very difficult for him to care for my mother, keep up with the farm, work his other job, and look after my two younger brothers, one of whom was only 15 years old.

My dad was a very loving, caring, and devoted husband and father, but he would obviously need plenty of help and support during this time. Both of my sisters were already married and had their own families to care for. One sister was expecting her first child and was living in the Phoenix area with her husband where they were serving as youth pastors. My oldest sister and her husband lived less than an hour away from my parents, but she had a young son who needed her attention. In spite of that fact, she was at my parents' home a great deal and did what she could during this trying time.

Meanwhile, I had moved to Tulsa, Oklahoma, to work and prepare to go to Bible school the following year. Because of my mother's illness, I decided to move back home to be with her and support my dad.

Both of my parents were very godly people. They had raised us in a wonderful Christian home and a great church. My entire family and our little church were all praying for my sweet mom.

Prior to my mother's illness, a friend had given me a copy of a book by a man named Kenneth E. Hagin. Even though I had grown up in a Pentecostal church only an hour away from Tulsa where Rev. Hagin's ministry was located, this was the first time I had ever heard of Kenneth E. Hagin or his newly begun RHEMA Bible Training Center. The truth of his message had so touched my life and spoken to my heart that I planned to attend RHEMA the following year.

My eyes were being opened to the truths of God's Word concerning our authority as believers and especially the fact that it is God's will to heal. During the time I helped care for my precious mom, I tried to share with her some of the insights I had received from God's Word.

My mother was a wonderful Christian woman. She loved the Lord with all of her heart, was a faithful church attendee, Sunday school teacher, tither, and giver to the Lord and others in so many ways. She and my dad were known and respected in our community for what they stood for and all of their kind acts and deeds. They were truly great examples of what Christians should be. Surely if God was going to heal anyone, it would be her!

My mom fought a valiant fight and did her very best to believe for her healing based on the knowledge she had of God's Word. But despite all of our efforts, she slipped into Glory on January 5, 1976, just four short months after her diagnosis.

In her final days and hours on this earth, it became apparent to all of us that she was growing more aware of "the other side" than she was of this earth. We could see that her affections were turning toward Heaven and her desire to depart was intensifying. The light of Heaven was ushering her into the loving arms of her precious Lord and Savior.

During the last few hours of her life, there was an awesome presence of God that filled her room and an undeniable peace. She had no fear. There was no struggle. She just fell asleep in Jesus. God met her where she was. She didn't have to take pain medication, and she died in her own bed, in her home of over 25 years, and surrounded by her adoring family.

Precious Is the Death of God's Saints

The Bible is certainly truthful concerning what is stated in Psalm 116:15: *"Precious in the sight of the Lord Is the death of His saints."* Even if a Christian dies from an ungodly sickness or disease, when their body begins to shut down and they take their final breaths, they are not tormented by the devil. Demons can't harass them. No! The angels of the Lord escort them to the other side.

Heaven is a real place, and death is just a shadow that we pass through to get to our eternal home. It is hard to feel badly for a Christian when they die at any age, if we have a revelation of where they have gone. The Apostle Paul said in Philippians 1:23, *"But I am hard pressed between the two. My yearning desire is to depart (to be free of this world, to set forth) and be with Christ, for that is far, far better"* (Amplified). Death is far better for the departed one, but those who are left behind must deal with their loss.

Even though I witnessed my mom's glorious homegoing and knew that she was free from pain and at peace, I was filled with questions and confusion as to why she had died instead of receiving her healing. Had we not prayed hard enough? Did we not believe strongly enough? Where had we missed it?

I didn't have the answers or full understanding of all that had transpired, but I knew it would be futile to blame God. He is never at fault and He never misses it. Too many people make the mistake of blaming the Lord for tragedies and situations they don't understand. There are even insurance policies that call tornados, hurricanes, and earthquakes acts of God. Nothing could be further from the truth!

God is not the author of disasters, tragedies, sickness, or disease. My limited knowledge of the Word of God and my strong personal relationship with the Lord Jesus assured me of His love and goodness. Thank God, I ran *toward* Him, not *from* Him.

Our Heavenly Father is faithful. He will meet us right where we are. Through the ministry of the Holy Spirit, He began to comfort and guide me into His perfect plan for my life. Let's read what He promised in His Word:

JOHN 14:16-17 (Amplified)

16 And I will ask the Father, and He will give you another Comforter (Counselor, Helper, Intercessor, Advocate, Strengthener, and Standby), that He may remain with you forever—

17 The Spirit of Truth, Whom the world cannot receive (welcome, take to its heart), because it does not see Him or know and recognize Him. But you know and recognize Him, for He lives with you [constantly] and will be in you.

In this same beautiful chapter of John 14, the Bible declares that not only is the Holy Spirit our Comforter, Counselor, Helper, Advocate, Strengthener, and Standby, but He is also our Teacher and the Giver of peace as well:

JOHN 14:26-27 (Amplified)

26 But the Comforter (Counselor, Helper, Intercessor, Advocate, Strengthener, Standby), the Holy Spirit, Whom the Father will send in My name [in My place, to represent Me and act on My behalf], He will teach you all things. And He will cause you to recall (will remind you of, bring to your remembrance) everything I have told you.

27 Peace I leave with you; My [own] peace I now give and bequeath to you. Not as the world gives do I give to you. Do not let your hearts be troubled, neither let them be afraid. [Stop allowing yourselves to be agitated and disturbed; and do not permit yourselves to be fearful and intimidated and cowardly and unsettled.]

When we enter into the arena of questioning, our peace is disturbed and we become agitated at God and others. It is also very emotionally unsettling if we don't know what to believe or who to trust.

As I struggled with my feelings concerning my mother's death, the Holy Spirit just kept gently bringing comfort and peace to me. When thoughts would come that caused me to question God's healing power, my peace was disturbed, so I knew those thoughts were not from God. That may sound simple and childlike, but isn't that how we are supposed to be in regard to believing God and His Word?

There was definitely a battle going on concerning my future. As I stated earlier, prior to my mom's illness, I had been planning to attend RHEMA Bible Training Center in the fall of 1976. After her death, I wondered if I would be able to lay hands on the sick with confidence and assurance and boldly declare that it is *always* God's will to heal. Once again, the Holy Spirit, Who is sent to lead and guide us and reveal to us the Father's will, came to my aid and assistance:

JOHN 16:13–14 (Amplified)

13 But when He, the Spirit of Truth (the Truth-giving Spirit) comes, He will guide you into all the Truth (the whole, full Truth). For He will not speak His own message [on His own authority]; but He will tell whatever He hears [from the Father; He will give the message that has been given to Him], and He will announce and declare to you the things that are to come [that will happen in the future].

14 He will honor and glorify Me, because He will take of (receive, draw upon) what is Mine and will reveal (declare, disclose, transmit) it to you.

There were many things that were still unclear to me, but somehow I had a strong knowing that I must still go to RHEMA. I had a good job and was saving my money. I thought I could delay attending for another year, but my heart was telling me, "Go *now*." It was hard to think of leaving my dad, but being the godly man that he was, he insisted that I apply for RHEMA and pursue the call of God that he knew was on my life.

My parents had taught all of their children that nothing was more important than being in God's perfect will. My dad also said that there was no higher honor on this earth than to be called into the ministry. Out of five children, three of us are in full-time ministry and the other two are very active in the ministry of helps in their churches. We all thank God for parents who encouraged us to obey God!

My Divine Destiny

After my application to RHEMA was processed and my acceptance was confirmed, my dad and I made a trip to Broken Arrow to secure a place for me to live. That was the first year that RHEMA was located at its current location, but they had not yet purchased the apartment complex across the street from the campus. This complex was rapidly becoming the ideal choice for incoming students, and many were already living there. It was the first place we looked and we both felt good about it. So the deposit was made and I had a place to live.

A few weeks later, as we were moving my belongings into the apartment, the manager made a comment to me about the young man who had recently moved into the apartment directly below mine. She told me that he, too, was attending RHEMA and maybe I should check on him. She said that he had moved in with very few possessions (in contrast to the abundance of furnishings in my apartment), and he didn't even have a car! So I bounded down the stairs and boldly knocked on my "door of destiny." As they say, "The rest is history!"

Mark and I have different accounts of that first meeting, but I can say that I had an immediate witness in my spirit that this was not a chance encounter. I also thought he was really cute! My southern hospitality may have overwhelmed him at first, but it didn't take long for him to get accustomed to some country cooking!

Mark and I were not only from different religious backgrounds, but we were raised in different parts of the country. He grew up in a good Catholic home in Minneapolis, Minnesota. Through no fault of his family, he had succumbed to the drug scene of the 1960s. He had experimented with drugs in high school but he became completely addicted in college. He finally dropped out in his sophomore year. It wasn't until the fall of 1974 that he hit rock bottom and discovered that he needed help to get free from his devastating addiction.

When Mark realized he couldn't master this challenge on his own, he went to the ones who loved him and would do everything in their power to help him—his parents. They managed to get him into a treatment center in Willmar, Minnesota, where he could receive help through the withdrawal process and support and counseling afterward.

Through sheer willpower and a strong desire to be free, Mark kicked the habit and was on the road to recovery. But inside there was still a deep emptiness. On March 17, 1975, he was invited to go to an evangelistic crusade. Even though he had no idea what that was, he gladly went. As the minister laid out the plan of salvation, Mark was thrilled with what he heard. He knew this was exactly what he needed to fill the aching void in his life. He was the first one to answer the altar call.

I believe Mark was supernaturally led by the Holy Spirit to stay in Willmar after he was released from the treatment center. In his quest for spiritual answers, he found a small group of believers meeting in a building near his house. As God continued to orchestrate his steps, a graduate of RHEMA came to pastor that little group of people. Mark devoured the Word of God and wanted more, so he decided he would attend RHEMA in the fall of 1976.

Isn't God awesome? At the same time that He was directing the steps of a girl in rural Oklahoma, He was moving on an ex-drug addict in Minnesota. I have often wondered how my life would have turned out if I hadn't overcome grief and stepped out to attend RHEMA, or if Mark had been too fearful to move to the "strange land of Oklahoma." We would have both missed out on God's best for us. It pays to obey the promptings in your heart, even if your head is screaming, "This doesn't make sense!"

Not only was my divine appointment with my wonderful husband waiting for me at RHEMA, but so were the answers to my spiritual questions. I will never forget the day that Rev. Hagin began to tell us the account of his sister's untimely death.[1] She had died in her fifties, and after her passing, he was caught up into Heaven and saw his sister talking with Jesus. She turned to him and told him not to feel badly that she hadn't received her healing—there were reasons.

She also told him to tell her children she would know when they made spiritual progress because in Heaven they are cheering us on in our race. *"Therefore we also, since we are surrounded by so great a cloud of witnesses, let us lay aside every weight, and the sin which so easily ensnares us, and let us run with endurance the race that is set before us"* (Heb. 12:1). Our loved ones who are in Heaven are part of that great cloud of witnesses.

According to Rev. Hagin's account, those who have gone on before us don't know or care about the natural things that happen to us, such as when we get a new house or buy a new car. But they do know what is happening to us spiritually.

I was elated to realize that my mom was aware that I had answered the call of God on my life and was in a good place to accommodate my spiritual growth. I was thrilled that she was part of that innumerable company of witnesses cheering us on from the grandstands of Heaven.

Rev. Hagin also shared a scripture with us that brought me a tremendous amount of peace. *"The secret things belong to the Lord our God, but those things which are revealed belong to us and to our children forever, that we may do all the words of this law"* (Deut. 29:29). The Holy Spirit spoke to Rev. Hagin and revealed to him that there were reasons his sister had not received her healing, but those reasons were between her and the Lord. And he was not to touch it anymore in his thought life.

That was exactly what I needed to hear, and from that day to this, I have never questioned the Lord again about my mom's death. And I have always endeavored to preach the full truth of the Word of God, which includes healing.

Retaliate in the Spirit!

Sometimes when we face a loss or think we have failed in a certain area, we shy away from that area or make excuses about why things happened the way they did. Neither response is correct. As I mentioned previously, we should follow Jesus' example and do what He did after his cousin John the Baptist was beheaded (Matthew chapter 14). It was unjust and unreasonable for John the Baptist to suffer such an awful death. If this had taken place today, it would have been a perfect case for a wrongful death suit.

When Jesus heard about the fate of John the Baptist, instead of lashing out at Herod, He did what we should do. He recognized the source of the attack as the devil and made the decision to go to the source rather than battle with flesh and blood. He retaliated in the Spirit and did damage to Satan's kingdom by going out and setting the captives free!

At a time when He probably would have preferred to be left alone, the Bible tells us that He was moved with compassion and healed the sick. (See Matt. 14:14.) That act of compassion and mercy did more harm to Satan's kingdom than anything He could have done in the natural toward Herod or his ungodly wife.

When we have been hurt or suffered a loss, the tendency is to withdraw, turn inward, and nurse our hurts or wounds. Certainly there is a time to heal, recover, and be restored. But we are not to despair to the point of withdrawing from the game of life.

Instead of being overwhelmed with our personal grief, at some point we must rise up and reach out to others just as Jesus did. Often when we reach out to help someone else, we receive our own healing and wholeness. The Bible says in Luke 6:38, *"Give, and it will be given to you: good measure, pressed down, shaken together, and running over will be put into your bosom. For with the same measure that you use, it will be measured back to you."*

God instituted the principle of "give, and it will be given back to you." It works in every area of life. If you need love, sow love. If you need joy, give some joy away. If you need healing in your body, pray for someone else who needs healing, and it will be multiplied back to you!

As this truth began to be branded on the inside of me, all fear and hesitancy left me. I knew I could boldly proclaim that Jesus not only died for our sins, but that the stripes upon His back were for our healing. Healing is part of our covenant rights as born-again believers. We do not receive it according to our personal experience or what we have done; it is based solely upon what He did for us.

I was confident of the course of action I must take, which was to retaliate in the realm of the Spirit against sickness and disease and its author, Satan. Over the past 30 years, my husband and I have laid hands on hundreds of people and seen many healed by the power of God. I am fully persuaded that my mother is part of that great company of witnesses in Heaven, and she is very much aware of all the people who have been born again, delivered, set free, and healed through our ministry. All the glory goes to our Lord Jesus Christ, and I thank Him for making me whole and ordering the steps of my life.

You see, God has ways that we cannot even comprehend to get His blessings to us and fulfill His plan for our lives. All that is required on our part is that we trust and obey Him. There's an old hymn that goes like this:

Trust and obey, for there's no other way

To be happy in Jesus, but to trust and obey.[2]

I am happy today in Jesus, my marriage, and my calling because I trusted and obeyed the Lord!

CHAPTER 5

Our Place of Refuge

Have you ever been enjoying a lovely outdoor activity on a seemingly beautiful day, when out of nowhere, a gulley-washer of a rainstorm hit? Where I grew up in Oklahoma, these types of storms are commonplace, especially in the springtime. Oklahoma is the ideal spot for cold air from the north and warm air from the Gulf of Mexico to collide. When this happens, the weather can go from sunny and clear to potentially threatening in a very short time. My daddy often told visitors to our fair state that if they didn't like the weather, just stick around. It would probably change soon!

If you have had the unfortunate experience of being caught outdoors unprepared when a downpour hit, what was the first thing you looked for? Most likely, you sought out shelter, a place of refuge, somewhere you could be protected from the storm. You may have found yourself running into a nearby building, dashing to your vehicle, or just trying to cover up with a raincoat or jacket. No one wants to get drenched by an unexpected torrential rain.

We don't enjoy being caught off guard by storms in the natural, and it isn't pleasant to have this happen in our spiritual walk either. The good news is, we have a place of refuge in God—a hiding place where we are safe from the howling winds and gathering storm clouds of life.

There are numerous passages in the Bible regarding preservation, many of which are found in the Book of Psalms. I want to share some examples with you. Psalm 86:2 says, *"Preserve my life, for I am holy; You are my God; Save Your servant who trusts in You!"* Another passage is found in Psalm 121.

PSALM 121:5–8

5 The Lord is your keeper; The Lord is your shade at your right hand.

6 The sun shall not strike you by day, Nor the moon by night.

7 The Lord shall preserve you from all evil; He shall preserve your soul.

8 The Lord shall preserve your going out and your coming in From this time forth, and even forevermore.

Isn't that encouraging? The Lord keeps us! One definition of the word *keeper* is custodian. Sometimes in a divorce there is a major custody battle to determine which parent the children will live with and who will be the primary caretaker or have custody of the children. The Lord is saying that He has won custody of our lives! We are no longer under the dominion or reign of the devil. Satan lost the custody battle for our souls. We are under the care and protection of the Lord Jesus Christ!

It is our responsibility to relinquish control of our lives to the Lord. To quote the words of a famous country and western song, we should be saying, "Jesus, take the wheel!" When we allow Him to be in the driver's seat of our lives, He isn't going to let us crash or drive over a cliff. This passage also promises us that we are under His protection and preservation, whether we are coming or going—today, tomorrow, and forever. I think that covers it all!

There is another scripture I want to examine which is found in the Book of Psalms as well. *"You are my hiding place; You shall preserve me from trouble; You shall surround me with songs of deliverance"* (Ps. 32:7). Isn't it interesting that God assures us of a hiding place, preservation, and deliverance? We wouldn't need these things if storms weren't coming, would we?

We all know that storms have come, are coming, and will come, but so what! We have a place of refuge in our God. He has promised to give us the direction and instruction we need to locate our safe place in Him. Let's read another passage from the Book of Psalms:

PSALM 32: 8-9

8 I will instruct you and teach you in the way you should go; I will guide you with My eye.

9 Do not be like the horse or like the mule, Which have no understanding, Which must be harnessed with bit and bridle, Else they will not come near you.

Our Heavenly Father has given us a promise in His Word that He would teach us, lead us, and guide us in the way we should go when we seek and inquire of Him. Where do you think He is going to lead us—into the wilderness, into dangerous territory, or into deep, dark pits? No! He has promised to show us the way *out* of these situations. We would do well to remember that God always provides a way of escape for us.

Our Father is the One with the answers, not the one sending the problems. He has awesome plans for our lives. They are not hidden *from* us, but *for* us. It is our responsibility to press in to God and discover the wonders of His Person and all the good things He has planned and made ready for us.

Don't Pattern Your Life After a Mule!

In order to walk in God's wonderful plans and dwell in that place of peace and protection, we must be open to receiving His instruction and correction. In the verse we just looked at from Psalm 32, what God wants to provide for us is clearly laid out. Then in verse 9, He cautions us about what we should not do. Let's read that verse again from *The Amplified Bible*. *"Be not like the horse or the mule, which lack understanding, which must have their mouths held firm with bit and bridle, or else they will not come with you."*

Mules are not the smartest animals, but they surely can be stubborn. If a mule decides he is not going to take another step, then operation "I shall not be moved" goes into effect. He will dig his heels into the ground, and no matter how hard his master pulls, it is almost impossible to move him. In extreme cases, the mule may even sit down on his back legs and refuse to get up. In essence, he is saying, "I don't care where you want me to go or what you may have in store for me, I am staying right here in this spot."

This passage is telling us not to pattern our lives after a stubborn mule. It is not a compliment when someone compares us to a mule. We do not want to be classified in that category.

Let's imagine for a moment what a mule might miss out on if he refuses to cooperate with his master. Suppose a farmer has a herd of cows and a mule, and he has kept them penned up in the barnyard all winter long. They have been given hay and feed every day, but they haven't seen or tasted fresh, green grass for several months.

Spring finally arrives, and the farmer is excited about opening the barnyard gate and letting his precious livestock enjoy a delightful and delicious treat. He unlatches the gate and begins leading the cows out into a beautiful, lush green meadow. The mule stretches his neck a bit, but he can't see where the farmer is headed, so he decides to stay in the brown, boring barnyard.

The farmer returns, coaxing and encouraging the mule to go with him. He tries everything he can think of, but the mule still refuses to move from the barnyard. With a look of disappointment and sadness, the farmer finally gives up and goes about his day, hoping the mule will change his mind and go through the open gate out into what God and nature have made possible for him to enjoy. Sadly, the mule remains in the barren barnyard all day long.

In the evening, the cows return to the barnyard with a hop in their steps and big smiles on their faces. Of course, they are happy cows because they are from California. Ha! The mule immediately gets depressed and asks the cows, "What did you do today? Where did you go? Why are you so happy?" Then he says, "The farmer did something special for you, didn't he? He loves you more than me. I have always known you were his favorites. He never treats me special."

The cows look at him and reply, "You foolish mule. The farmer tried to get you to go with us, but you refused. The things we partook of today could have been yours, too, if you had just been willing to be led into the green pastures."

Too many of God's people are acting like that mule. He has prepared wonderful paths for their lives, but they refuse to follow His promptings. They won't let Him lead them into the place of His provision or the position of His protection. Finding that place in God requires trust as is pointed out in the next two verses of Psalm 32:

PSALM 32:10-11

10 Many sorrows shall be to the wicked; But he who trusts in the Lord, mercy shall surround him.

11 Be glad in the Lord and rejoice, you righteous; And shout for joy, all you upright in heart!

Some of the grief and sorrow we experience in our lives could come because we have not trusted the Lord. Or perhaps we have not obeyed His promptings when He was trying to get us to a place of refuge from the storms of life.

We all get off track now and then, but we can jump right back onto the path of provision with just a few small tweaks and adjustments. When we trust the Lord and let Him instruct, teach, and guide us, we will find there is much to be glad about and great cause for rejoicing. His plans and paths are full of *goodness*! Won't you let Him lead you into greener pastures today?

CHAPTER 6

Can These Dead Bones Live?

We have all had the opportunity to let go of a dream or vision, lose hope, or say, "This is never going to come to pass. I guess this vision is dead forever!" Or how about the experience of giving up on a relationship? Have you ever been there? That relationship seems to be in the same condition as Lazarus was in John chapter 11—so dead that he "stinketh" by now!

When we find ourselves facing something that seems to be so dry and dead that it's past being revived, we can take heart and receive valuable insight and encouragement from the wonderful biblical account in Ezekiel chapter 37, where Ezekiel found himself in a valley of dry bones. But before we look at that story, let's establish Who is the Author of life and who is the author of death.

John 10:10 says, *"The thief [the devil] comes only in order to steal and kill and destroy. I came that they may have and enjoy life, and have it in abundance (to the full, till it overflows)"* (Amplified).

The devil is the destroyer. He is the author of death. He can't produce life because there is none in him.

The reverse is also true. God is the Author of life. When we have God—the Giver of life—on the inside of us (Someone on the inside working on the outside), the life of God inside us will transform our bodies, minds, finances, and every other area of our lives.

Whatever God touches, life flows into it. Whatever the devil touches, death is the result. I have good news today. No matter how grave or grim our situation may be, one touch from God can turn it around. One breath from God can bring resurrection power into death-filled situations. One word from the Lord can make all the difference for us.

Has God ever spoken to you? Have you ever been in a service where you were desperate for an answer, the Word of God came forth, and you received the answer you needed? The Word of God has *life* in it, and it will make a difference in your life.

The last part of Acts 3:19 in *The Amplified Bible* says, "*times of refreshing (of recovering from the effects of heat, of reviving with fresh air) may come from the presence of the Lord.*" Reviving, recovery from the effects of heat, and refreshing all come from the presence of the Lord. The word *revive* literally means "to return to life or consciousness, to impart new health, vigor, or spirit into, to restore to use." God is reviving His Church.

There was a time when our local church went through a season of prayer that I believe with all of my heart totally revived us. We had become lax and devoid of the life of God in some areas. He came in and breathed, afresh and anew, His breath all over those areas. New health and new vim and vigor were imparted into our church. I encourage you to receive His breath of life today in your circumstances!

What does a doctor do when somebody is dead? He tries to resuscitate them. What does that mean? It means to revive them or bring them back to life. If the medical profession can bring a physical body back to life, how much more can God invade the areas of our lives that the devil is trying to fill with death and breathe life back into them? There is no pit too deep, there is no hole too dark, and there is no trouble too great for the life of God to bring change into it.

I like the scripture in Psalm 138:7. We need to remember this verse when we're in difficult situations, especially when it seems that the devil is trying to creep in and cause death and destruction. The psalmist said, *"Though I walk in the midst of trouble, You [God] will revive me."* Hold on to that word, no matter what's going on around you. God will revive you. And then it goes on to say, *"You will stretch out Your hand Against the wrath of my enemies, And Your right hand will save me."* That's a wonderful promise from the Lord!

Remember, we can always call on His Name. He said, "Call on Me. I'm a very present help in time of trouble." (See Ps. 46:1.) When we speak His Word, the life of God will go forth and He will stretch forth His hand to deliver us. No matter what we're going through He said, "Call on Me, and I will revive you. I will refresh you. I will lift you up."

In other words, He's God when we're on the mountaintop, and He's God when we're down in the valley. Wherever we are, we can't get away from the presence of God. But we have to let Him be God in our lives.

The Dead Bones Were in the Valley

My question for you today is the same question God asked Ezekiel when he stood in the midst of that valley filled with dry bones. The Lord said to him, *"Can these bones live?"*

(Ezek. 37:3). In other words, no matter what you or someone you know is facing, is there ever a cutoff time when something is just too dead that it can't be revived?

We're going to see in this wonderful passage of scripture that the answer to that question is no. God is the God Who brings life into death-filled situations. Let's begin reading in verse 1 of Ezekiel chapter 37: *"The hand of the Lord came upon me and brought me out in the Spirit of the Lord, and set me down in the midst of the valley; and it was full of bones. Then He caused me to pass by them all around, and behold, there were very many in the open valley; and indeed they were very dry"* (vv. 1–2).

Let's look at these two verses more closely. I find it interesting that the dead bones were in the valley. They weren't on top of the mountain. We all like the mountaintop experiences in God. I've had a lot of them in my life. I love to be on the mountaintop.

What do I mean by mountaintop experience? I'm talking about those times when you're riding high spiritually. God is pouring dreams and visions into your spirit. You're so full of passion to serve Him that it seems there's nothing you can't do. You're saying, "Oh God, You've revealed Your truth to me, and the Word of God is so alive to me. Every morning when I wake up, my heart is communing with You." And you're not saying those things by faith. You're actually experiencing them. You're on a spiritual mountaintop.

Well, guess what? Vision doesn't die on the mountaintop. Attacks don't come when you're on the mountaintop. This scripture says that God showed the prophet all of these dead, dry bones *in the valley*. It was an "in the valley" experience.

Now, I'm not a negative, woe-is-me kind of preacher, but life happens. Our Christian walk is not always on the mountaintop. My husband, Mark, and I have been at this for a long time. There are times when we get up to minister the Word of God and it's so anointed. Then there are other times when we begin to minister the Word and we don't feel a thing. But we have to do it by faith. We have a joke that we share at times like those. We say, "I hope that wasn't Dry Hay Ministries. We don't want to change the name of our church to Dry Hay Church."

Oftentimes you have no idea why it's that way. You're still walking with the Lord in the same way you always have. You're still praying. You're still reading your Bible. But sometimes the feeling just isn't there. The mountaintop experience just isn't there.

What are we going to do in those times? Are we going to quit? Are we going to say, "Where did God go? I thought I was saved, filled with the Holy Ghost, and doing what I was supposed to do. But I don't feel a thing. I don't get goose bumps anymore." That happens to all of us at times. That's the valley kind of experience. We don't want to go there, but we all *do* go there sometimes.

Just know this. If you're in the valley right now, there is a mountaintop just ahead. You're going to get right back up there again. Don't stay in the valley. That's the key. When you're in a valley experience, don't camp out there, and don't choose to live there.

In Psalm 23:4, the psalmist David said, "*Though I walk through the valley of the shadow of death. . . .*" Don't you think it's interesting that the shadow of death wasn't on the mountaintop? It was in the valley. So don't get discouraged if you find yourself temporarily in the valley. And don't mail out any change-of-address cards. No, this is temporary. It's "passing through the valley" time. You're going to get through it. You're going to find yourself back on the mountaintop again.

Just keep doing what you know to do. Keep walking by faith. Keep praying by faith. Keep reading the Word by faith. Keep making your confessions by faith. It won't be long until you're right back up, spiritually. Don't be moved by the valley.

Sometimes we feel as if our lives are a heap of dead, dry bones. We cry out, "Lord God, nothing is working. Everything is falling apart." But we shouldn't be too concerned when that happens. We have to keep pressing into God and know that He is the great "bone collector." T.D. Jakes has an awesome message called "The Bone Collector," and it's about those times when we think our lives are full of dead, dry bones. God can take those lifeless bones and put them all back together and make something beautiful of them.

Really, it doesn't matter what you're looking at right now. It's doesn't matter how dry and dusty those bones may be. This passage from Ezekiel says the bones weren't just dead. They were dry. Think about it. It's kind of gross, but there wasn't one ounce of flesh on them. Nothing was left on the bones. That tells us that they had been dead for a long, long time.

Let me ask you a question. Does it matter how long your dream may have been dead? Does it matter how long there hasn't been any life in your finances? Does time matter to

God? When Jesus went to the tomb of Lazarus did He say, "Oh, I misunderstood. He's been dead four days? The third day was the cutoff day. After three days nobody can be raised from the dead." (See John chapter 11.)

No, time doesn't matter to God! No matter how long you've been standing, no matter how dead that dream or vision may seem, let God breathe life back into it. If you call on Him, give Him entrance, and pray in the Holy Ghost, the Spirit of God will come into any situation.

Jesus conquered death, hell, and the grave, and there is no time limit for Him to come in and restore your dreams. There is no time limit for Him to come in and restore broken relationships. There is no time limit for Him to come in and breathe fresh life into the area of your finances.

It doesn't matter how much debt you have or how long you've been in debt. God doesn't say, "Wait a minute. You've been in debt *way* too many years. You've gone past the cutoff date. There's no hope." God is the Author of life. He's the One Who can take those dead, dry bones at any stage and bring life back into them.

'It's Not Looking Good for the Bones Today'

In verse 3 of Ezekiel chapter 37, God is speaking to the prophet: "*And He said to me, 'Son of man, can these bones live?' So I answered, 'O Lord God, You know.'*" I like Ezekiel's response here. He said, in essence, "It's not looking good for the bones today, God. Have you seen them? They're really dead and dry." But notice that he didn't say, "No way, dude! Can't you see how dead and dusty these bones are?" He said, "Lord, You're the One Who knows."

That reminds me of what Mary said when the Holy Ghost asked her, "Will you have this Son [Jesus] for Me?" (See Luke chapter 1.) It was a difficult situation that she found herself in. But she did not say, "No." Instead, she said, "How are these things going to be?" She literally said, "*Let it be to me according to your word*" (v. 38).

That reminds me of Ezekiel's response here: "Lord, I don't know if these bones can live, but You know. And I'm going to trust You. I'm going to do what You tell me to do."

Let's read more of this amazing story:

EZEKIEL 37:4-6

4 Again He said to me, "Prophesy to these bones, and say to them, 'O dry bones, hear the word of the Lord!

5 Thus says the Lord God to these bones: "Surely I will cause breath to enter into you, and you shall live.

6 I will put sinews on you and bring flesh upon you, cover you with skin and put breath in you; and you shall live. Then you shall know that I am the Lord." ' "

Here is a beautiful example of what we need to do when we are facing death-filled situations. We need to get into the presence of God and we need to say, "Lord, what should I do? I want to cooperate with the Spirit of God. I want to hear and obey what You are saying to me."

God did not say to Ezekiel, "I'll take care of everything," although we know He could have done that. God wants us to cooperate with Him. He has designed things so that mankind has the opportunity to work with Him. He wants us to have the opportunity to use our faith.

So He was saying to Ezekiel in this passage, "Yes, dead bones are dry, and yes, I can bring life back into them. But I need your voice. I need your faith. I need you to say what I tell you to say."

We know that God created this earth. We know that Jesus is Lord. But there's an enemy here, and Adam sold us out to him. We, as human beings, are the ones who have authority in this earth. God needs us to cooperate with Him. He needs us to declare what He has declared in His Word. So He is saying here, "Ezekiel, you have to open your mouth. You have to speak to these dead, dry bones."

It's a trick of the enemy when we are facing difficulty to try to get us to shut our mouths. Why? Because he knows that when we speak the Word of God, life is expressed, and light goes forth while darkness is pushed back. Satan will tell us, "Oh, you've got a sore throat. You can't speak the Word now. You don't feel like praying now. You don't want to strain your voice." He tries to get us to keep our mouths shut when we should be opening our mouths and speaking life into the very atmosphere of our homes.

And what does Satan do when we should keep our mouths shut? He comes along and tells us to open our mouths. Why does he do that? He knows that when we open our mouths at the wrong time and say the wrong things, we're speaking death and darkness into the atmosphere of our lives.

For example, let's say something happens between you and your mate, and you get ticked off. The devil will tell you, "You really need to give them a piece of your mind. You need to tell them exactly how they made you feel. Just get it off your chest." And then you spew out all of these words of anger and strife.

What does that do? It doesn't clear the air. Instead, it contaminates the air with death and darkness. That's Satan's tactic. But God is teaching us through this scripture to say what He tells us to say, not what the devil wants us to say.

In verse 7, Ezekiel said, "*So I prophesied as I was commanded.*" Did you know that our words are carriers? Our words are containers. They paint pictures. I heard one minister say that our words are like a thermostat. They control the atmosphere of our lives. They set limits. They establish boundaries. When you set a thermostat, the temperature can rise or drop in a room or house.

Likewise, our faith will rise to the level of our confession. Whatever level we set our words, the faith on the inside of us will produce to that level. If we want our faith to go higher, then we need to change our words and make sure they are in line with the Word of God.

Notice that the Spirit of God did not say to Ezekiel, "Just go ahead and talk about what you see with your natural eyes. Go ahead and tell Me how you feel about those dead, dry bones. Tell Me if you think they can live." No, God told him exactly what to say, and Ezekiel had to open his mouth and declare what the Spirit of God told him to declare.

God knows everything. He knows what's going on with your child. He knows what's going on at your job. If you'll ask Him, He'll give you the right words to pray and the right words to say over those situations. As you speak those words, barriers will come down. Situations will change. A rebellious child's heart will be softened.

If we just fly off the handle and say a bunch of fleshly, carnal things, it won't change those dead situations. But when we have utterance from the Lord, it's awesome! And it will make a tremendous difference!

You don't have to be a preacher behind the pulpit to have utterance from the Lord and an anointing to say the right words. God will give you the right words. He will give you divine utterance, and it will have entrance into people's lives. He will cause a door to be opened into the hearts of your loved ones, even if their spirits have been closed to you before. When will He do it? When you pray in the Holy Ghost and say, "Lord, I put a guard over my mouth. Help me only to say what I feel prompted in my spirit to say."

All of us have people in our lives who need help. We can see from their lifestyles that they are suffering the consequences of their bad choices. It can be a temptation to tell them everything they're doing wrong and why all of this tragedy is happening to them. But that won't help them.

God knows what will help them. One word from Heaven can change a person's heart. One word from Heaven can open someone's spirit to the Gospel and to Jesus. Let's be carriers of life. Let's speak with the unction of the Holy Ghost, and He will change people and situations.

A Noise and a Shaking

Now I want us to look at the next few verses of this powerful story.

EZEKIEL 37:7-8

7 So I prophesied as I was commanded; and as I prophesied, there was a noise, and suddenly a rattling; and the bones came together, bone to bone.

8 Indeed, as I looked, the sinews and the flesh came upon them, and the skin covered them over; but there was no breath in them.

Let's camp out for a moment at verse 7. When Ezekiel prophesied, when he said what he was commanded to say, there was a noise and a shaking. Regardless of what we do or do not see in the natural, things happen in the realm of the Spirit when we pray and declare God's Word. If our eyes and ears were open to that realm, we would see and hear a shaking and a noise. We would see that the chains the devil has used to try to bind people are being shaken loose.

When a shaking occurs in the realm of the Spirit, people are shaken loose from the devil's grip and the blinders fall off their eyes. May God open *our* eyes and ears to what He is doing in the unseen realm!

I believe the Lord is telling us, "I have heard your cries. I have seen your tears. Your prayers have given Me entrance. They have given Me license to work in that situation—to work on the heart of that loved one. Don't be discouraged by what you may not see. I am working behind the scenes. Oh, it's coming! It's coming to pass! They're coming in, in the Name of Jesus, and that situation is turning around."

When God begins to shake the devil's kingdom, there's a whole lot of shaking going on. And there's not a thing Satan can do about it. He cannot hold people captive when God reaches down and shakes the very regions of hell and the damned. The captives are set free.

The devil is not your loved ones' god! They might be serving him right now, but when we pray to the God Who is greater, the Greater One shows up on the scene. It happens in the realm of the Spirit before we ever see it in the natural. Sometimes we just need to rejoice and call it done by faith.

"Hook up with Me," says the Lord. "See things the way I see them. I see those loved ones already in the Kingdom of God. I see that situation already turned around. I see those prayers and petitions already answered. See it the way I see it. Come up higher and see things from My perspective." Powerful things are happening in the realm of the Spirit when we pray. There's a whole lot of shaking going on!

The Bible says in Haggai 2:7, *"'And I will shake all nations, and they shall come to the Desire of All Nations, and I will fill this temple with glory,' says the Lord of hosts."* Not only is God shaking situations and shaking the captives free, but He is also shaking nations. Entire nations are having encounters with the power of God. There are notable prophets who have said that there are nations that will be won in a day.

Our natural mind says, "How can that be?" God can show Himself strong. He can shake a nation that's been bound by false religion so that everybody sees signs and wonders in the heavens. Jesus Himself may even show up and reveal Himself to the leader of that nation in such a powerful way that he or she comes out publicly and says, "I've been wrong. Jesus is Lord." It will shake a nation if some of its leaders have encounters with and supernatural visitations from the Spirit of God.

Not only are nations going to be shaken, but things are also going to be shaken right there where you live. Do you really believe that? You haven't written off your hometown, have you? You haven't said, "This is a godless, sinless, perverse area. God can't do anything here. I'm just going to hold out to the end."

No, our hearts must say, "God, if You're going to do something anywhere in the earth, You're going to do it here. You're going to do it for the sake of the righteous. We're pleading our case. We're standing on the Word. Father, shake our cities that the people will know that there is a God. Fill Your churches with Your glory and Your healing power." He is doing it, and He's doing it right where you live!

Let's finish reading this passage in Ezekiel.

EZEKIEL 37:9–10

9 Also He said to me, "Prophesy to the breath, prophesy, son of man, and say to the breath, 'Thus says the Lord God: "Come from the four winds, O breath, and breathe on these slain, that they may live."' "

10 So I prophesied as He commanded me, and breath came into them, and they lived, and stood upon their feet, an exceedingly great army.

It was a progression. First Ezekiel prophesied to the dead, dry bones, and flesh came upon them. At that point, they looked pretty good. They looked like human beings again. But they were still not alive. Then God said to him, "You need to prophesy to the wind." When he prophesied to the wind, the breath of God blew into that valley, and the members of that great army became living souls.

Do you remember when God created Adam? He looked pretty good, didn't he? He was a man, created in the image and likeness of God, but he was lying on the ground, dead. He looked okay, but it wasn't until God breathed into his nostrils that he became a living soul. (See Gen. 2:7.)

I have a word for you today. Maybe your situation is not filled with death. Maybe it looks pretty good. But if it's not full of the life of God, don't stop pressing in. Don't settle for second best. Get the *whole thing.* Get *all* that God has for you. Don't stop short. Just cry out, "Lord, I know that things are pretty good and You've done a lot in my life. But I want more! I want it all!" Let Him do everything that He wants to do in your life. Don't fall short of enjoying God's very best!

Ezekiel said that as he prophesied, the slain bodies of the soldiers came to life. They *"stood upon their feet, an exceedingly great army"* (v. 10). Are you part of the army of the Lord God? Do you want to serve the Lord with all of your heart? God is looking for an army that will invade the devil's domain. He's looking for an army that will pull people out of darkness. He's looking for an army that will rise up and take back what the devil has tried to steal from the Church.

God didn't stop with that army just looking good. He didn't stop when they had just a little bit of life in them. He kept breathing His life into them until they became His army, until they became usable.

God is looking for people He can use. He wants to take care of everything in our lives. He wants to meet all of our needs. But He wants us to get beyond that and look outward and be an army that will reach out to help other people. God wants to breathe life into our death-filled situations, and He wants us to be carriers of His life to hurting humanity. Will you be part of His "exceeding great army?"

CHAPTER 7

Never Say Die—Persevere!

One thing that always occurs when we have been going through a trial or difficulty for a long period of time is that we experience the temptation to quit. For some reason, we think a lapse of time means that what we're believing for isn't going to come to pass. But, remember, God doesn't operate on our timetable. He is not limited by the dates on a calendar or the instrument we call a clock. It is foolish to try to confine God to these things. It's also foolish for our joy and faith to be weakened because of them.

When our faith and trust are in the Lord, we should know that we will not be disappointed. In the game called life, it is our bat and ball, and our Heavenly Father is the umpire. He is the One calling the plays, and He won't call us out, nor will He call the game over until *we win*!

Did you ever play games as a kid where you asked for a do-over? If you had nice friends or friends who also needed do-overs, that request was usually granted. Our Father is a loving Father. He will give us as many do-overs as we need! It isn't over until it's over, and it's not over until we win!

It takes perseverance and tenacity to stand until we receive the desired end results. This principle is found throughout the Word of God and is available to all of us.

The word *persevere* means "to persist in or remain constant to a purpose, idea, or task in the face of obstacles or discouragement." A thesaurus offers many synonyms for *persevere* in the verb form, including "carry on, keep going, go for it, hold fast."[3] Or as I would say in my southern vernacular, "Never say die!" Don't you love that? It denotes fighting until the very end.

The word *perseverance* gives us even further insight. Some of the meanings are "stick-to-itiveness, tenacity, steadfastness, commitment, and singleness of purpose." Unfortunately, a lot of people in our day and age, even some Christians, know very little about persevering, being steadfast, or sticking to anything.

Many have adopted the attitude, "I'll do it if it's easy. I'll stay in that relationship as long as it brings me pleasure. If not, I'll just change spouses. I'll just change jobs. I'll play musical churches. I'll stay in that church as long as it doesn't cost me anything and there's no pressure on me to do anything. I don't want to go to a church that talks about commitment, perseverance, or stick-to-it-iveness. Hey, this is the 21st century! We're free. We can do whatever we want to do."

As believers, the Bible refers to us in Isaiah 61:3 as *"trees of righteousness, the planting of the Lord."* Let's read that entire verse from the *New King James Version.*

ISAIAH 61:3

3 "To console those who mourn in Zion, To give them beauty for ashes, The oil of joy for mourning, The garment of praise for the spirit of heaviness; That they may be called trees of righteousness, The planting of the Lord, that He may be glorified."

A tree can't grow unless it remains planted. I have a good friend on our church staff who has been serving with us for a number of years. She has faithfully served in various capacities in the church. Anything we have asked her to do, she has done, cheerfully and well.

I love something she always says: "I just grow where I am planted!" Isn't that a great philosophy to live by? We shouldn't always have the attitude that we're looking for the easiest way out. Instead, we should be discovering God's way. His way is always higher and better, and it is a sure foundation that leads us into victory every time.

These verses from First Corinthians chapter 15 contain a powerful message for us:

1 CORINTHIANS 15:57-58 (Amplified)

57 But thanks be to God, Who gives us the victory [making us conquerors] through our Lord Jesus Christ.

58 Therefore, my beloved brethren, be firm (steadfast), immovable, always abounding in the work of the Lord [always being superior, excelling, doing MORE THAN ENOUGH in the service of the Lord], knowing and being continually aware that your labor in the Lord is not futile [it is never wasted or to no purpose].

Have you ever heard the saying "No grass is gonna grow under my feet"? Or have you heard the song "Papa Was a Rolling Stone"? These are not verses in the Bible. The Holy Ghost did not inspire somebody to write them.

We are to be firm. We are to be steadfast like First Corinthians 15:58 says. We are going to further the cause of Christ. We are going to live for the Kingdom of God. We're going to be good witnesses. We're going to be good soldiers. We're going to keep on wearing the armor of God. We're going to be immovable, unshakable, and firm. We're going to be like a planted tree!

We should always give God more than enough. We should never have the attitude, "Well, we're just doing this for the Lord. Kids, get your broken toys. Get your raggedy clothes. And look in the cabinet for all the food that has an expired date. Let's take those things to the church." No! First Corinthians 15:58 said that we should do "more than enough" in the service of the Lord.

One of the names of our God is El Shaddai, "the God Who is more than enough." If we want God to bless us with more than enough, we ought to be willing to give Him more than enough. We shouldn't have the attitude, "Well, just a little dab of service to God will do." No! We ought to have the desire to do more in the Kingdom of God every day.

Every day we ought to say, "Help me, Jesus, to be a bigger blessing today than I was yesterday. Show me someone I can give an encouraging word to. Lord, I want to do more for You today than I did yesterday." We should desire to excel. We should want to do far beyond the average or ordinary. We should be people who persevere, who stick with things, and who won't quit at the first sign of difficulty. We won't quit on God, His Word, or His Church!

Put on Your Armor

Ephesians 6:11 has a lot to say about persevering and standing. *"Put on God's whole armor [the armor of a heavy-armed soldier which God supplies], that you may be able successfully to stand up against [all] the strategies and the deceits of the devil*" (Amplified). We don't have to design and make our own armor. We don't have to make our own shield of faith. God gives us all the equipment we need. He supplies our armor. His part is to provide it. Our part is to put it on.

Once we have our armor on, what are we able to do? We can successfully stand. Stand against what? Against all the deceits and strategies of the devil. How many of them? Just a few? No, all! The last time I checked, *all* meant *all*. It means everything. There's nothing—no strategy of the enemy that can come against us—that God has not already given us the victory over.

That verse then says, "*. . . and the deceits of the devil.*" One of the devil's major tools is deception. Of course, he loves to deceive the lost. He loves to blind their eyes to the truth of the Gospel so they won't become born again. But his deception doesn't stop with those who aren't born again. He loves to deceive Christians too. And the kind of Christian he really likes to take advantage of is the pseudo-spiritual one.

He will come along and say, "You're facing the big crisis this time. It's a huge, gigantic trial, and it calls for you to fast for 120 days." Now, fasting is certainly scriptural, but it can become a work of the flesh when we try to do something in our own strength to earn an answer to our prayers. People sometimes do foolish things, such as going on extended fasts without the leading of the Lord, and they wind up deceived and flakey. They start hearing all sorts of voices that aren't from God.

Don't allow yourself to be forced or pushed into doing anything. The Holy Spirit leads. He doesn't drive. If you are feeling pressured to fast, maybe you should just go out and eat a cheeseburger and enter into rest! Besides, we will never change anything or anyone by our own works or in our own strength.

Be strong in the Lord and in the power of His might, stay with the Word, follow after peace, and you won't be deceived. Ephesians 6:12 says, *"For we do not wrestle against flesh and blood, but against principalities, against powers, against the rulers of the darkness of this age, against spiritual hosts of wickedness in the heavenly places."* This verse also points out who our real enemy is. It is the devil, not people.

It's important to know who your enemy is. Yes, we are in a fight, but we do not wrestle with people. People can and do yield to the devil, but we should realize that our real battle is not with flesh and blood, but with the evil spirits that influence people.

You may have a difficult relative, somebody you work with, or perhaps even your boss, who is very ungodly and loves to tell filthy jokes or preach from the "Book of Cuss." They'll do anything to harass or try to intimidate you.

You probably shouldn't say anything to them out loud, but under your breath, you can take authority over the foul spirits that operate through them. You can go into your office or some other private place and say, "You foul spirit, I command you to be quiet in my presence. I don't have to listen to that filth. I don't have to hear that kind of language." Use your God-given authority. Deal with spiritual issues in the Spirit. Don't get angry with people. Deal with the source. The source is the devil who influences people to act like that.

Now let's read on in verse 13 of Ephesians chapter 6, *"Therefore take up the whole armor of God, that you may be able to withstand in the evil day, and having done all, to stand."* It doesn't say to take up your favorite piece of the armor of God. We are to put on the *whole* armor. That means we are to wear every piece.

Once we have the armor on, what are we supposed to do? Withstand! The notes in the *New Spirit-Filled Life Bible* say something interesting about the word *withstand*. It is taken from the Greek word *anthistemi*, and that is the root word for *antihistamine*. *Anti* means "against" and *histemi* means to "cause to stand." The verb suggests vigorously opposing, bravely resisting, standing face-to-face against an adversary. It implies standing your ground.[4]

Just as an antihistamine puts a block on a runny nose, the word *anthistemi* tells us that with the authority and spiritual weapons granted to us by the Lord, we can withstand and block any evil force. We can put a block on any of the weapons of the devil. We have the authority to stand up and say, "In the Name of Jesus, no you don't! This attack stops right now, in the Name of Jesus! Devil, I withstand you, and no weapon formed against me is going to prosper."

We have to take a stand. The authority has been given to us, but we must rise up and stand on the Word of God and say to the devil, "Stop, in the Name of Jesus!" If we're going to successfully do that, we're going to have to do what it says in the next few verses:

EPHESIANS 6:14-17

14 Stand therefore, having girded your waist with truth, having put on the breastplate of righteousness,

71

15 and having shod your feet with the preparation of the gospel of peace;

16 above all, taking the shield of faith with which you will be able to quench all the fiery darts of the wicked one.

17 And take the helmet of salvation, and the sword of the Spirit, which is the word of God.

This gives us more details about the armor God has given us. Notice it covers the entire front section of the body. Let's start with what is covering our heads first. He said our heads will be covered with the helmet of salvation.

I love the entire Body of Christ, but many Christians stop putting on their armor right there. All they put on is the helmet of salvation. That's wonderful, and of course, the helmet of salvation is the most important part of our armor. Everything begins when we are born again. But it doesn't end there. If we don't put on the rest of the armor, we're "streaking" in the realm of the Spirit. Unfortunately, there are a lot of "spiritual streakers" in the Body of Christ. They have on their helmet of salvation, but the rest of their bodies are totally unprotected.

You don't get up in the morning and say, "I don't feel like getting dressed today, so I am just going to put on a hat and go to Starbucks," do you? You would be arrested if you walked around the streets of your city, only wearing a base-ball cap. There are laws protecting the public from completely exposed flesh. Maybe those laws should be enforced a little more today!

There should be a lesson in that for us, as Christians. If it is against man's law for us to expose our natural bodies, it is against God's law, His Word, for us to expose our spirit man. That's why we need to put on the whole armor of God!

The Rest of the Armor

What are the other pieces of this armor that we are instructed to wear? The breastplate of righteousness is one very important piece of our armor. This is one that a lot of Christians struggle with. They yield to the deception of the devil and buy into the religious lies that tell them they are unworthy worms. After all, the Bible says, our *"righteousnesses are as filthy rags"* (Isa. 64:6 KJV).

Yes, it is true that all of us were unworthy before we met the Lord, and our own righteousness *is* like filthy rags. But Jesus has made us righteous, and He is the One Who clothes us with beautiful, new robes of righteousness. *"For He made Him who knew no sin to be sin for us, that we might become the righteousness of God in Him"* (2 Cor. 5:21). Let's turn to another passage from the Book of Isaiah.

ISAIAH 61:1-3

1 "The Spirit of the Lord God is upon Me, Because the Lord has anointed Me To preach good tidings to the poor; He has sent Me to heal the brokenhearted, To proclaim liberty to the captives, And the opening of the prison to those who are bound;

2 To proclaim the acceptable year of the Lord, And the day of vengeance of our God; To comfort all who mourn,

3 To console those who mourn in Zion, To give them beauty for ashes, The oil of joy for mourning, The garment of praise for the spirit of heaviness; That they may be called trees of righteousness, The planting of the Lord, that He may be glorified."

Jesus has made us righteous. We shouldn't be intimidated or negligent about putting on the breastplate of righteousness which He has provided for us. If we are suffering from unrighteousness consciousness and refuse to put on our breastplate of righteousness, then the whole front of our body is exposed to the attacks of the enemy. How he loves to attack us with guilt and condemnation!

If you don't know who you are in Christ and are not assured that your sins and mistakes are cleansed by His precious blood, then you will be continually beaten up by the lies of the devil. I encourage you to pick up your breastplate and resist those thoughts of unworthiness!

How about your loins? Are they girded about with truth? What is the truth? John 17:17 says, *"Sanctify them [purify, consecrate, separate them for Yourself, make them holy] by the Truth; Your Word is Truth"* (Amplified).

The Word of God is the truth. It's the source of our strength. Knowing the Word gives us power to stand in difficult times. I think that is why this part of our armor goes on our loins. *Webster's Dictionary* defines the loin area as "the part of the side and back between the ribs and pelvis; the area of the groin or thighs; the reproductive organs."[5]

The Word of God covering our loins will produce results and cause us to stand the test of time. We should look at Ephesians 6:13–14 again to get the full impact of what it's saying to us: "*. . . having done all, to stand. Stand therefore, having your loins girt about with truth*" (KJV). What causes us to be able to stand? It is the truth—the Word of God in our hearts—that gives us supernatural strength to stand.

How about our feet? Are we supposed to be running around barefoot? Absolutely not! Ephesians 6:15 in *The Amplified Bible* says, "*And having shod your feet in preparation [to face the enemy with the firm-footed stability, the promptness, and the readiness produced by the good news] of the Gospel of peace."* We are to face each day and each battle in life with peace. The peace of God causes us to be firm-footed, stable, and fixed.

What produces that kind of peace? It's knowing that our Father cares for us and being confident in what He has promised us in His Word. This requires faith. That is why the shield of faith is emphasized in our armor. Ephesians 6:16 says, *"above all, taking the shield of faith with which you will be able to quench all the fiery darts of the wicked one."*

Notice the phrase *above all*. It highlights the importance of our faith. There are too many Christians who don't know anything about using their faith or confessing the Word of God. Christianity is called "The Great Confession." Confession is a major part of how we become born again. Romans 10:9–10 states, *"If you confess with your mouth the Lord Jesus and believe in your heart that God has raised Him from the dead, you will be saved. For with the heart one believes unto righteousness, and with the mouth confession is made unto salvation."*

Confessing Jesus as our Lord brings us eternal life. Confessing what the Word of God says about our situation will bring us victory. Our flesh will always try to get us to talk about the problem and speak doubt and unbelief. But lifting up our shield of faith will produce the answer. Our shield of faith is also vital in quenching *"all the fiery darts of the wicked one"* (v. 16). Satan loves to bring discouragement and make us think God has forgotten about us. But we can resist his lies, raise up the shield of faith, and declare what the Word says.

God's Word is referred to in Ephesians 6:17 as the *"sword of the Spirit."* Almost every piece of our armor is something we put on our bodies. But the shield of faith and our sword—the Word of God—are to be used as weapons. There is another place where the Word of God is referred to as a sword.

HEBREWS 4:12 (Amplified)

12 For the Word that God speaks is alive and full of power [making it active, operative, energizing, and effective]; it is sharper than any two-edged sword, penetrating to the dividing line of the breath of life (soul) and [the immortal] spirit, and of joints and marrow [of the deepest parts of our nature], exposing and sifting and analyzing and judging the very thoughts and purposes of the heart.

The Word is sharp. It is quick, alive, and it will penetrate any situation and bring life-giving power. Pick up your God-given sword and cut the devil down to size. Don't allow his lies to rule and reign over you. You rule and reign over them with the powerful Word of the Living God.

There is one last thing that I want to mention about the armor of God. The armor covers or protects the front side of our bodies. There's nothing to protect our backsides. What is that telling us? We are not to be on the defensive. We are to be on the offensive! We don't want to be like the lady who testified during a Sunday night church service, saying, "I just want you to know I've had the devil on the run all week." Everybody was about to get excited when she continued, "I've been running, and he's been chasing me." That isn't anything to be happy about.

We're not supposed to be chased by the devil all the time. We're supposed to put him on the run with the sword of the

Spirit—the Word of God! God wants us to resist the devil and he will flee from us (James 4:7). We ought to have the attitude, "No, devil, I'm not going to quit. You're not going to knock me out of this race. If you want a piece of me, come on. I'm wearing my armor. I'm strong in the Lord. If it's a fight you want, it's a fight you're going to get!"

That's the kind of attitude we ought to have! Devil, I'm not tucking my tail and running from you and I'm not turning my back. I'm standing on God's promises, and they will not fail. I'm standing my ground even though the howling winds of fear and doubt assail. I'm standing on the promises of Christ, my King![6]

I love something Pastor Kenneth W. Hagin always says: "I cannot be defeated and I will not quit." That should be the theme of our entire lives!

CHAPTER 8

Last Man Standing

Life is a journey. On any journey you're going to experience wonderful times, but you will most likely also experience some not so great times. Have you ever noticed how traveling can bring out the worst in people? Whether you are flying or driving to a destination, at the end of the day, you are usually tired and hungry, not to mention in much need of a hot shower and comfortable bed. But those basic needs are not always satisfied without conquering some obstacles and overcoming a few bumps in the road.

We all know what it is like to have our faith and patience tested by a rude waiter or waitress, a hotel clerk with an attitude, a hostile driver, or a very unhelpful or uncompassionate airline employee! Without even asking, I am sure every one of you reading this book has failed in dealing with those kinds of "tests" from time to time just as I have. But I am confident that you have also passed some of those tests. When you did, you were probably delighted with the sense of victory that swept over your soul. It was a testimony to God's grace and peace in you, which are greater than the forces and pressures trying to rob you of His peace!

Have you ever considered the fact that the first four letters of the word *testimony* spell t-e-s-t? You can't have a testimony without passing a test. The great news for believers is that every test we face is an open book test—all the answers are

79

found in the Bible! There isn't anything we face in life that Jesus has not already given us the ability to conquer and triumph over. Neither is there anything we face that is unique to us.

The enemy tries to get us to believe that each one of us is a "special" case and no one else has ever encountered what we are going through. But that is not true. First Corinthians 10:13 says, *"No temptation has overtaken you except such as is common to man; but God is faithful, who will not allow you to be tempted beyond what you are able, but with the temptation will also make the way of escape, that you may be able to bear it."*

Let's also take a look at this verse in *The Amplified Bible*:

1 CORINTHIANS 10:13

13 For no temptation (no trial regarded as enticing to sin), [no matter how it comes or where it leads] has overtaken you and laid hold on you that is not common to man [that is, no temptation or trial has come to you that is beyond human resistance and that is not adjusted and adapted and belonging to human experience, and such as man can bear]. But God is faithful [to His Word and to His compassionate nature], and He [can be trusted] not to let you be tempted and tried and assayed beyond your ability and strength of resistance and power to endure, but with the temptation He will [always] also provide the way out (the means of escape to a landing place), that you may be capable and strong and powerful to bear up under it patiently.

The devil has no new devices or tactics. He may change the characters and rearrange the plot, but it is the "same old, same old" with him. He has the same purpose and plan every time—to bring discouragement and defeat into our lives. But thank God that He gives us the victory in every and all circumstances. He will always provide *"the means of escape to a landing place,"* a place of safety, peace, and victory.

One of my favorite passages of scripture and a keynote verse for my life and ministry is found in Second Corinthians 2:14—*"Now thanks be unto God, which always causeth us to triumph in Christ, and maketh manifest the savour of his knowledge by us in every place"* (KJV). How often does God cause us to triumph? Always! In *The Amplified Bible,* that same verse says, *"But thanks be to God, Who in Christ always leads us in triumph [as trophies of Christ's victory] and through us spreads and makes evident the fragrance of the knowledge of God everywhere."* God leads us where? Into triumph.

That verse didn't say that God leads us out into a dry, barren place. It didn't say that He leads us into traps, snares, and plots of the devil so Satan can beat up on us. No! God always leads us where? Into triumph. Into victory. How often does He cause us to triumph? Always!

The word *always* is a great word. Sometimes it helps us to get the full impact of a word by looking at its definition in the dictionary. Two definitions of *always* given in the dictionary are "at every instance"[7] and "for all time."[8] I like that! Jesus said, *"For all time I'm going to cause you to triumph. For all time you are a trophy of My grace and goodness."*

Another definition of *always* is "forever." Forever! So when you see the word *always* in the Bible, you can say, "That means forever as well." When I saw that, it reminded me of this wonderful scripture found in Psalm 119:89, *"Forever, O*

Lord, Your word is settled in heaven [stands firm as the heavens]" (Amplified). How long is the Word settled? Forever!

We serve an unchanging God and a God Who cannot lie. When He speaks something or declares something in His Word, when He declares something over your life, it is forever settled. Then verse 90 of Psalm 119 goes on to say, *"Your faithfulness is from generation to generation; You have established the earth, and it stands fast"* (Amplified).

We can always count on God. He is a faithful God. He is a reliable God. He is not a man that He should lie. If He has said it, it will come to pass. It is forever settled in Heaven. His faithfulness stands forever!

I am not sure if you're familiar with this poem or not, but when I was in high school we studied a poem by Edgar Allan Poe entitled "The Raven." It was really a rather dark poem, when you think about it. The poem's narrator encounters a raven on a cold, dark night and begins to speak to it and ask it questions. The raven's answers are always, "Nevermore."

The devil is like that big, black bird. He'll say to you, "Nevermore. You're not going to get your healing—nevermore. Not this time. You're not going to be able to pay your bills—nevermore. Not this time. Your kids are never going to line up—nevermore. Not this time. That was the last time God is going to pull you out of that mess—nevermore!"

But do you know what? There's another bird in the Bible (if you don't mind me using that analogy). It's the dove—the dove of the Holy Spirit. Every time the devil says, "Nevermore," the dove, the Holy Spirit, says, "Always."

Anytime you hear the voice that says, "Never—it will never happen for you. Your dream will never come to pass. You're never going to be free from that bondage. You're never going to prosper financially," there's another voice you ought to listen to. That voice is right there on the inside of you—the voice of the Spirit of God. Every time a "never" comes to your mind, let that other voice rise up and say, "Always. I always triumph in Christ Jesus."

The Greatest Winner Lives in Us

When we stay connected with the Lord and in tune with His Spirit, when we keep our eyes on the Word and are attentive to God's voice, guess what? We cannot fail and we will not be defeated. Why? Because the greatest Winner Who ever lived, lives on the inside of us!

Against all odds, Jesus Christ rose up victorious over death, hell, and the grave. Did He have opportunities to quit? Of course He did. But His attitude gives us the example we should follow. Winners never quit and quitters never win!

You are a winner in Jesus, so I encourage you to act like Him and refuse to quit. According to the Bible, temptations, tests, and trials come to steal our faith and rob us of our joy. The devil loves to make us think that he has won and we are completely defeated by his attacks. But when he takes his best shot and throws his hardest blow and we continue to persevere and stand on the Word, he is the one who gets discouraged!

There is a verse I want to look at in the Book of Job. Most people think Job is only a story of tragedy and defeat. But it is really about overcoming those things and receiving complete restoration. We will look at that in detail in another chapter, but the verse I want to focus on right now is Job 19:25, *"For I know that my Redeemer lives, and He shall stand at last on the earth."*

I know my Redeemer lives. Aren't you glad that you serve a risen Savior? Aren't you glad that He's not in some grave or tomb? People who worship Buddha and Mohammed know exactly where their gods are buried. But our Redeemer is not in the tomb where He was buried. Our Redeemer lives. That's the difference between Christianity and every other religion.

Yes, Jesus died, but He didn't stay dead. He rose up from that grave, and He is in Heaven right now, seated at the right hand of the Father. And what is He doing? He's enforcing our redemption. The blood forever speaks, and it's saying, "They're redeemed!"

When the devil, the accuser of the brethren, comes into the throne room of the Father and starts accusing us, all Jesus has to do is point to the blood and say, "The blood says they're redeemed. The blood says their sin is washed away. It's been removed as far as the east is from the west." And if we've confessed it, the devil can't bring it up. It's gone. It's under the blood.

Another interesting phrase in this passage that stands out to me is this: *"He [Jesus] shall stand at last on the earth."* Jesus is the last Man standing. It reminds me of a scene from an old western movie. Can't you just see two gunfighters out in the street with their hands on their gun holsters, ready to draw? The outcome is determined by who is the quickest to draw his gun and shoot his opponent. The fastest gunman will be the last man standing.

In the battle of the ages, Jesus was the last Man standing. He was temporarily knocked down. He was in the grave for three days. But He was still the last Man standing. He rose up out of that grave, and when He rose up, He stood up. When He stood up, He put His foot on the devil's neck. But it didn't end there! He's still the last Man standing. And He said to the Church, "I will make your enemies your footstool." (See Matt. 22:44.)

No matter what comes against you, no matter how many times you might get knocked down, you just keep getting up! You can declare by faith, "I might be temporarily knocked down, but I'm coming up. Mr. Devil, I'm going to be the last man standing here. You're the one who's going down—down into the eternal pit." And the devil is going to be down for eternity while we're going to be up!

Remember, God always causes us to triumph. He always causes us to stand. We're going to stand on His promises. We're going to stand on our redemption. And we're going to rise up every single time. "*Do not rejoice over me, my enemy; When I fall, I will arise; When I sit in darkness, The Lord will be a light to me*" (Micah 7:8). It's not over until it's over, and it isn't over until we take our last breath or until we quit. So don't quit!

We will always be victorious and the last man standing when we keep our eyes on the Lord and refuse to be moved by the circumstances around us. I like something I heard a man of God once say, "God has power to shower." He can turn a potential "meltdown" into a miracle and shower you with unexpected blessings from unusual and unlikely places.

CHAPTER 9

A Strong Spirit Will Sustain You

If we are going to experience restoration in our lives, our hearts must be clean before the Lord. It *does* matter what is on the inside of us. If we're harboring offenses, bitterness, jealousy, resentfulness, and unforgiveness, we will hinder the power of God from flowing into us and through us. We don't want anything to plug up the flow of the Spirit of God!

In the natural, is it important to have a strong, healthy heart? All of us want our "tickers" to be in good shape, don't we? The condition of our physical hearts will be a major factor that determines how long we live on this earth. It is really unwise to not be mindful of the things we are doing—or not doing—that can have an ill effect on our hearts.

If this is true of our physical hearts, how much more should we be mindful of the condition of our spiritual hearts (our spirit man)? Proverbs 4:23 says, *"Keep and guard your heart with all vigilance and above all that you guard, for out of it flow the springs of life"* (Amplified).

When we are under pressure from the cares of this world and the attacks of the enemy, some of the first things we usually let slip are our intake of the Word and our fellowship with the Father. Our flesh will tell us that we are too tired to pray or read the Word. It will encourage us to just "chill." Of course, there is absolutely nothing wrong with relaxing, but when we give our flesh an inch, it will try to take a mile. Before we know it, several days or maybe even weeks will have passed since we picked up our Bibles or had a good, long talk with the Father.

Maybe you have heard the saying, "One week without the Word makes one weak." Just as our physical bodies require good nutrients and vitamins to function the way God created them to function, our hearts require input from the Word of God to remain strong. Jeremiah 15:16 says, *"Your [God's] words were found, and I ate them; and Your words were to me a joy and the rejoicing of my heart, for I am called by Your name, O Lord God of hosts"* (Amplified).

The Word of God stirs up joy, and it also gives strength to our inner man. When we are strong on the inside, we will be able to withstand and conquer all the attacks that come our way. If we're strong on the inside it will show up on the outside. There is an awesome scripture in the Book of Proverbs that confirms what I am saying here. *"The strong spirit of a man sustains him in bodily pain or trouble, but a weak and broken spirit who can raise up or bear?"* (Prov. 18:14 Amplified). What sustains a man or woman? A strong spirit!

If you have been putting the Word of God into your heart on a regular basis, what comes out when the enemy pokes at you will be power, peace, and strength. Hell may be breaking loose all around you, but if you've got the Lord on the inside and you're built up from feeding on the Word, it doesn't matter what's going on around you. You're going to stand firm. You're going to stand tall. You're going to be fixed, settled, and established—sustained on the Word of the Living God.

Darts may be coming from every direction, but the wisdom of God is rising up big on the inside of you. The Holy Spirit is leading, guiding, and directing your steps into victory and safety. You know you are not alone, and you are aware of how to tap into God's supernatural help. You are not trying to do things in your own strength or ability. This is not a natural battle that you are fighting.

Let's take a person who's trained in the military, such as a Navy SEAL or a Green Beret. They are at the top of their field. They may have outrun and out-fought everyone and perhaps even dodged more bullets than anyone else. They may be very agile and trained in how to take cover when they're under attack. But even a soldier—or anyone else who has undergone extensive physical training—is still not a match for spiritual darts and attacks.

This has nothing to do with how agile or physically fit you are. It has everything to do with how strong you are on the inside. A 90-pound, 90-year-old grandma who is full of the Word, full of faith, and full of power can whip the devil every single time. Why? Because she's strong on the inside. Who and what is on the inside of you makes all the difference.

Are you strong on the inside? Are you infused with the inner strength that comes from the Spirit of the Lord? If you are, then you will not faint in the time of trouble or the day of adversity. Proverbs 24:10 says, *"If you faint in the day of adversity, your strength is small"* (Amplified). *The Message* Bible says, *"If you fall to pieces in a crisis, there wasn't much to you in the first place."*

Let's look at some characteristics of a man with a strong spirit. What does he do when trouble comes? Psalm 112 gives us a clear picture of what a man whose heart is settled on the Word of God is like. Verse 1 defines the person who is referenced in this entire passage. *"Praise the Lord! Blessed is the man who fears the Lord, Who delights greatly in His commandments."* The criteria for being a blessed man is being someone who fears, reveres, and worships the Lord—someone who delights in His commandments.

When was the last time you picked up the Word of God and said, "Yum, yum, delicious and nutritious. This is yummy"? That's what we should be saying about the Word of God all the time. The psalmist David said that God's Word is sweeter than *"honey and the honeycomb"* (Ps. 19:10). That's talking about delighting in His commandments. That's the kind of man Psalm 112 is describing.

Now let's read on in verse 2, *"His seed shall be mighty upon earth: the generation of the upright shall be blessed"* (KJV). Do you want your seed to be mighty upon the earth? Do you want the generations after you to be blessed? Then be a man or woman who fears and reverences the Lord and delights in His commandments. Verse 3 goes on to say, *"Wealth and riches will be in his house, And his righteousness endures forever."*

It doesn't say poverty, lack, gloom, despair, and agony are in his house. No, it says wealth and riches are in his house. He is abundantly supplied and funded, and he has every need met because he's seeking first the Kingdom of God.

Matthew 6:33 says that if we seek first the Kingdom of God, then all the other things we need will be added to us. All of these things includes material blessings.

God is a good Father. He wants our needs to be met. He desires for His children to have abundance in their households: abundance of peace, joy, love, health, strength, and also abundance of material blessings! God is not opposed to His children having possessions, but He *is* opposed to possessions having a grip on His children. We are not to seek after things. We are to seek Him!

Another characteristic of the person described in Psalm 112 is found in verse 4, *"Unto the upright there arises light in the darkness; He is gracious, and full of compassion, and righteous."* That's awesome, isn't it? What is that verse telling us? When the world is full of darkness, distress, and turmoil, the righteous are going to have peace, joy, and life. It might be dark all around us, but we will have light because we are the children of light.

Do you remember when the children of Israel were in the land of Egypt and Pharaoh refused to let them go? God instructed Moses to warn Pharaoh that each time he refused to let the children of Israel leave Egypt there would be a new plague in the land. (You can read about all the plagues and God's deliverance in Exodus chapters 7–12.) One of the plagues was intense darkness. The account of the plague of darkness is found in Exodus chapter 10:

EXODUS 10:21-23

21 Then the Lord said to Moses, "Stretch out your hand toward heaven, that there may be darkness over the land of Egypt, darkness which may even be felt."

22 So Moses stretched out his hand toward heaven, and there was thick darkness in all the land of Egypt three days.

23 They did not see one another; nor did anyone rise from his place for three days. But all the children of Israel had light in their dwellings.

The Bible says the darkness was so thick in the land of Egypt that the people couldn't even see each other. This was true everywhere except in the land of Goshen, where the children of Israel lived. There was light in the land of Goshen.

Maybe you've heard about a special kind of weapon that can shut down all the power in a certain area. It can reportedly shut down all the computers and everything else that's run by electrical power. I don't believe we're going to experience something like that, but even if we did, I believe the people of God would still have power and light in their dwelling places.

If God has to supernaturally cause the glory of the Lord to shine in my house, I'm going to have light in the darkness. If He has to keep my tank full of gas when all the gas stations are empty, I'm going to have gas in my car. There is going to be a difference for the blessed man or woman. There's going to be a difference for someone who seeks first the Kingdom of God. Darkness may be all around us, but we can still have light in our lives.

A Fixed Heart Is Not Afraid

I want to continue looking at verses 5–8 in Psalm 112 from *The Amplified Bible*:

PSALM 112:5-8

5 It is well with the man who deals generously and lends, who conducts his affairs with justice.

6 He will not be moved forever; the [uncompromisingly] righteous (the upright, in right standing with God) shall be in everlasting remembrance.

7 He shall not be afraid of evil tidings; his heart is firmly fixed, trusting (leaning on and being confident) in the Lord.

8 His heart is established and steady, he will not be afraid while he waits to see his desire established upon his adversaries.

What is this saying? A fixed heart is not afraid. A fixed heart is trusting in, leaning on, and confident in the Lord our God. Certainly we have opportunities to be overwhelmed. Evil reports may be bombarding us on a regular basis. Perhaps the company we work for is downsizing and there is constant talk of layoffs. Maybe our child didn't get that scholarship he or she applied for. Perhaps we received a bad report from the doctor.

I don't know what kind of bad news or evil report you might have heard, but I do know that you do not have to be moved by it. As long as you are strong on the inside, you will win on the outside!

We all know that evil tidings are out there. We all know that bad news abounds. There are some people who, instead of making a to-do list or a shopping list, make an evil report list. They freely rattle off all the evil things they can think of, everything that's wrong in the world, and everything that could go wrong. They worry about things that will probably never happen!

But you're not one of those people! Your heart is fixed. Your heart is steady. Your eyes are focused on the Lord. You're not looking at the trouble. You're not looking at the lack. You're not listening to all the voices out there. You are firmly fixed and rooted and grounded in Him.

When those negative things begin to bombard your heart, if your spirit man is strong it will sustain you. Your spirit man will rise up and keep you steady. You'll be immovable, unshakable, unwavering, and unchangeable because you're hooked up with a God Who does not change.

Doesn't the Bible say that Jesus Christ is the same yesterday, today, and forever (Heb. 13:8)? It doesn't say that Jesus is the same unless the economy goes bad or Jesus is the same unless the swine flu shows up. No, it says that Jesus is *always* the same. We're hooked up with the right Source. We're on the Rock. We can go to the Rock that is higher than us, and our Rock does not roll!

This world's system is a shaky foundation. If we have our trust and confidence in the world, we're going to be severely disappointed. The earth is rocking and reeling. Anything that can be shaken will be shaken. But one of the verses we just looked at said that a man who is on the firm foundation will not be moved. *"He will not be moved forever . . ."* (Ps. 112:6 Amplified).

If you've been feeling a little shaky or unsteady, I would advise you to check your foundation. Make sure that no termites have entered in. Make sure there's no strife. Make sure there's no doubt. Make sure there's no worry trying to creep into your foundation. Definitely make certain there's no rotten lumber.

What's rotten lumber? Works of the flesh such as pride or the attitude that says, "I've built this great kingdom. Look at this career I've had. Look at all of these possessions I've attained. I, I, I, me, me, me." That's rotten lumber.

You can't build anything good with rotten lumber. It has termites in it. It will collapse. It might look good for a little while on the outside. But at the first sign of a wind or storm, at the first opportunity for a meltdown, everything will come falling down.

Can you see how important a strong foundation is? A structure can be constructed quickly, and it may look like a strong, secure house. But if the foundation is shaky, the house won't be steady. It won't stand the storms of life.

The Bible gives us a beautiful illustration about two people who each built the same type of house. The only difference between their houses was the foundation. This story is found in Matthew chapter 7. Let's begin reading with verses 24–25: " *'Therefore whoever hears these sayings of Mine, and does them, I will liken him to a wise man who built his house on the rock: and the rain descended, the floods came, and the winds blew and beat on that house; and it did not fall, for it was founded on the rock.'* " The Bible calls this man wise. What happened to his house when the storm came? It stood. Why? Because it was built on a solid foundation, as solid as a rock. As a matter of fact, it was a rock!

Then the Bible goes on in verses 26–27 to describe a foolish man: " *'But everyone who hears these sayings of Mine, and does not do them, will be like a foolish man who built his house on the sand: and the rain descended, the floods came, and the winds blew and beat on that house; and it fell. And great was its fall.'* " Notice the similarities between the wise man and the foolish man. They both heard the same thing—the Word. But the wise man acted on what he heard while the foolish man didn't.

Isn't it interesting that the storm is described in exactly the same way in each of these narratives? It was the same storm. The rain wasn't falling harder and the winds weren't blowing stronger against the foolish man's house. Neither was the wise man exempt from the storm. The storms of life come to everyone's house.

What determines the outcome when we are in the midst of a storm? It is the foundation upon which we have built. The wise man and the foolish man may have even used the same material to build their houses, but there was a vast difference in what they each built upon. There is no comparison between sand and rock.

If you grew up in Sunday school, you may remember a song we sometimes sang about this parable entitled "The Wise Man Built His House." It went something like this: "The wise man built his house upon the rock. The rains came down and the floods came up, and the house on the rock stood fast. The foolish man built his house upon the sand. The rains came down and the floods came up, and the house on the sand went 'splat.' "

The strength of our spiritual foundation is connected to what is in our hearts. If we will see to it that our hearts are fed a continual diet of the Word of God, then Proverbs 18:14 will become a reality in our lives: "*The strong spirit of a man sustains him*" (Amplified). We will not faint or falter when the storms of life come.

When we are strong on the inside, it will affect our speech. The Bible says in Matthew 12:34, "*Out of the abundance of the heart the mouth speaks.*" That is a scary thought when you consider some of the vile things you have heard people say! What in the world have they been feeding on? I don't think I want to expound on that, but I'm sure you get the message.

There is life and strength in the Word of God. If that is what you put into your heart, then that is what will come out of your mouth, especially in difficult times. I once heard a man of God say something that has stuck with me for many years—"If you will feed your heart faith when it looks like you *don't* need it, your heart will feed your mouth faith when you *do* need it."

Joel 3:10 says, *"Let the weak say, 'I am strong.'"* Our words are important, and they play a huge role in helping us recover what the enemy has tried to steal from us. When our spirits are strong, our words will be strong and full of power. They will help shape our world and bring change to our circumstances. So let's keep our spirits strong and our words in line with God's Word. Then we will prosper and be of *great* benefit to His Kingdom.

CHAPTER 10

Don't Forget to Praise

When we are in the midst of a battle, it is easy to talk about the problem and magnify the difficulty. But the Bible is clear about Who deserves to be talked about and Who we should magnify. Even though our problems and difficulties can seem like the biggest thing in our lives, they are not bigger than God. We must learn to magnify Him above all else.

What happens when we put something under a magnifying glass? It appears bigger than it does to the naked eye. When we magnify the Lord, He doesn't actually get any bigger. He is the same yesterday, today, and forever. He isn't going to get any more powerful, stronger, or greater than He already is. But when we magnify Him, our perception of Him expands. He becomes larger in our eyes. I think we would all be wise to put God under a magnifying glass so we can get a clearer picture of all of His wonders and attributes!

The Bible tells us that we should magnify the Lord. "*O magnify the Lord with me, and let us exalt His name together. I sought (inquired of) the Lord and required Him [of necessity and on the authority of His Word], and He heard me, and delivered me from all my fears*" (Ps. 34:3–4 Amplified).

This verse instructs us to magnify and exalt the Lord, to seek and inquire of Him. He is the One Who is worthy to be praised. He is the One Who has all of our answers. He is the

One Who will provide a way of escape from any adverse circumstance. He is our Deliverer. He is not our problem, nor is He the one who sent the difficulty.

There are way too many Christians who get their praises mixed up. Perhaps you grew up in a church like I did which often had testimony services on Sunday night. I heard a story about one such service where a woman wasn't testifying of God's goodness. Instead, she was going through her list of trials. She ended her sad story with, "The devil has been after me all week. Bless his holy name."

I am sure she didn't realize she had confused her praises and was blessing the name of the devil, but unfortunately she is not alone in that category. Many Christians are unknowingly guilty of the same mistake. They are praising God for sickness and disease, poverty and lack, and tests and trials that magnify the devil's power. That is wrong!

God isn't sending the tests and trials, and the devil isn't all-powerful. As we stated earlier in this book, difficulties do come to all of us, but when they do, we don't receive them as being from our loving Heavenly Father or get mad and blame Him for them. We look up and expect Him to intervene and show us the way of escape!

Let's look at First Thessalonians 5:18, *"Thank [God] in everything [no matter what the circumstances may be, be thankful and give thanks], for this is the will of God for you [who are] in Christ Jesus [the Revealer and Mediator of that will]"* (Amplified). Notice the phrase *"in* everything." It didn't say, *"for* everything." There is a vast difference between those terms.

We are to praise God even when we don't feel like it or when the circumstances don't deserve our praise. Why is that? It is a statement to God. It is a statement of our faith and trust in Him, His goodness, His vastness, and His ability to take any bad situation and turn it around. That is His specialty. He is a Master at fixing any disaster!

When we make the choice to rejoice and magnify the Lord, it gives Him entrance into our affairs and an opportunity to show Himself strong. It also steals the lies of the devil and causes Satan to pack up his bag of tricks and flee. Praise magnifies God above all the plans, plots, and strategies of the devil.

There's a scripture in Psalm 8:2 (KJV) which says that praise stills the enemy and the avenger. The devil is full of pride. The devil is full of himself. That's what got him into trouble in the first place. Because he said, "I will be like the Most High God. I will exalt myself." (See Isa. 14:14.) Pride is what caused Satan's downfall. He craves praise and worship. But only the Father and the Lord Jesus are worthy of our praise and admiration.

When we refuse to magnify the devil or exalt him, it deflates his pride. We should refuse to say things like, "Ooh, the devil is so big. He's so bad. Look what he did. Ooh, ooh, ooh, the devil."

We should not reverence the devil. We shouldn't give him any kind of attention except to resist him and remind him of what a loser he is! The only message we have for the devil is this: "You're under my feet." So anything we have to say to him, we need to write on the bottom of our shoes!

When we don't magnify Satan, when we don't exalt him, guess what? He won't stick around. He doesn't like to be ignored. He doesn't like to be put in his place. That truth alone should inspire us to become proficient in our praise to our Father.

You see, praise is a powerful force that stills the enemy. I love this acrostic I heard several years ago on the word praise:

P -Pushes back the enemy

R -Releases God's power

A -Gives us access to God's presence

I -Increases our capacity to receive from God

S -Sustains us in tough times

E -Establishes and encourages our hearts

The Power of Prayer and Praise

I love the Bible. I grew up in Sunday school, hearing the stories from God's Word as a little girl. And I will have to say that even as a little girl, one of my favorite Old Testament Bible stories was the account of King Jehoshaphat and the children of Israel and how God caused them to triumph over their enemies. This biblical account of the power of prayer and praise is found in the Book of Second Chronicles.

2 CHRONICLES 20:1-2

1 It happened after this that the people of Moab with the people of Ammon, and others with them besides the Ammonites, came to battle against Jehoshaphat.

2 Then some came and told Jehoshaphat, saying, "A great multitude is coming against you from beyond the sea, from Syria; and they are in Hazazon Tamar" (which is En Gedi).

Jehoshaphat received a bad report telling him that all of these enemy armies were coming against the people of Judah. Now he was a man of God, but he was also a man. He was human just as we are human. I'm sure he was tempted to be afraid just as you or I would have been.

If you had all of these giant "ites" coming after you, wouldn't you be tempted to be afraid? You might say "Oh no, not me. I'm a man of faith and power." Yeah, right! Then why are you afraid of the dark or the neighbor's barking dog?

Anyway, this was a life and death situation. In the natural, the people of God were greatly outnumbered and had no viable defense. But Jehoshaphat didn't stay in fear. He didn't try to figure out a battle strategy with the leaders of his army. The Bible tells us exactly what he did and what we should do when we are facing impossible odds.

2 CHRONICLES 20:3–4 (Amplified)

3 Then Jehoshaphat feared, and set himself [determinedly, as his vital need] to seek the Lord; he proclaimed a fast in all Judah.

4 And Judah gathered together to ask help from the Lord; even out of all the cities of Judah they came to seek the Lord [yearning for Him with all their desire].

Jehoshaphat knew where their help came from. He was also aware that all of Judah needed to seek the Lord together. There are seasons when we must empty the depths of our souls and the secret rooms of our hearts to our Father and our Father alone. Certain intimate details of our conversations are for His ears only. But there are other times that require the faith and prayers of all the saints of God. This account in Second Chronicles was one of those times.

This Was No 'Doubt and Unbelief' Meeting

When Judah came together it was not a "doubt and unbelief" meeting. This was not a time when they started talking about how big the Moabites were. They weren't spewing out negative or fearful words. They weren't saying, "You know what I heard? These are big, bad dudes. They killed this group of people. They terrorized that group of people. We're all going to die!" No, the Bible tells us in the next few verses what they said and did:

2 CHRONICLES 20:5-11 (Amplified)

5 And Jehoshaphat stood in the assembly of Judah and Jerusalem in the house of the Lord before the new court

6 And said, O Lord, God of our fathers, are You not God in heaven? And do You not rule over all the kingdoms of the nations? In Your hand are power and might, so that none is able to withstand You.

7 Did not You, O our God, drive out the inhabitants of this land before Your people Israel and give it forever to the descendants of Abraham Your friend?

8 They dwelt in it and have built You a sanctuary in it for Your Name, saying,

9 If evil comes upon us, the sword of judgment, or pestilence, or famine, we will stand before this house and before You— for Your Name [and the symbol of Your presence] is in this house—and cry to You in our affliction, and You will hear and save.

10 And now behold, the men of Ammon, Moab, and Mount Seir, whom You would not let Israel invade when they came from the land of Egypt, and whom they turned from and did not destroy—

11 Behold, they reward us by coming to drive us out of Your possession which You have given us to inherit.

The people were reminded of all the miraculous things God had done in bringing them into the Promised Land. Even though nothing had changed in their outside world—even though the Moabites, the Ammonites, and all the other "ites" were still waiting to attack them—something began to change on the *inside* of them.

When you start magnifying God, rehearsing past victories, and talking about how big the Lord is, something starts changing inside you. When you remember how He healed your body, how He's been faithful to your family, or how you've never seen the righteous forsaken nor his seed begging for bread (Ps. 37:25), something will change on the inside of you.

It doesn't matter what's going on around you, on the outside. What matters is what's going on in your heart. When your heart is fixed on the Word of God, your faith will be equal to anything and everything the enemy may throw at you.

We must learn to live out of our hearts and not our heads. That is what Judah did. They had their eyes on the Lord. It was all about Him. They were looking to Him for their next step. They weren't trying to figure out how they could possibly win this battle, in the natural. They called upon the Lord concerning the strategy to win this battle.

I love what verse 12 of Second Chronicles chapter 20 says, *"O our God, will You not exercise judgment upon them? For we have no might to stand against this great company that is coming against us. We do not know what to do, but our eyes are upon You"* (Amplified). They recognized right away that they had no might in their own physical being. They couldn't whip this army in their own strength. They were far outnumbered. They said, "We don't know what to do!"

Have you ever been there? Have you ever said, "Lord, I don't know what to do?" But don't stop there. Don't stop with, "I don't know what to do." That's not all that Jehoshaphat said. Yes, he recognized that this was beyond his intellect and resources. But he also said, "Our eyes are on You, Lord." Don't you love that phrase?

I know I have been in that position many times, but how reassuring and liberating it is to look up to Heaven and declare, "My eyes are on You, Lord. I may not know how. I may not know when. But I know You will do it again. You will find a way to fix this for me."

If you'll stay completely dependent on the Lord, steadfast and immovable, unshakable on the Word of God, He will always show you what to do. He will always give you direction. The Bible says, "*The steps of a good man are ordered of the Lord*" (Ps. 37:23). But He usually gives you the steps one at a time. He probably won't show you the whole picture or plan all at once. Just step out into the light you have today, and the grace for tomorrow will be there when you need it!

Our Children Need to See God in Action

Let's follow the progression of this awesome biblical story. "*And all Judah stood before the Lord, with their children and their wives*" (2 Chron. 20:13 Amplified). Notice that they didn't hire babysitters so they could seek the Lord, undisturbed by their children. No! They brought their little ones to the prayer meeting.

When we're in a time of need or crisis, we ought to share our faith and what we are believing God for with our children. We should let our children experience the victory of answered prayer! Let them see that God is the One Who provides for us.

When they begin to see His abundant provision and mighty acts as small children, they'll never turn away from Him. They will know that He's the Most High God. Why would they want to go away from Him if He's delivered them every time their family has called on Him? Witnessing answered prayer will assure our children of God's love and watchful care for them. We need to let them see Him in action!

Let's look at what happened as this powerful story unfolded:

2 CHRONICLES 20:14-15 (Amplified)

14 Then the Spirit of the Lord came upon Jahaziel son of Zechariah, the son of Benaiah, the son of Jeiel, the son of Mattaniah, a Levite of the sons of Asaph, in the midst of the assembly.

15 He said, Hearken, all Judah, you inhabitants of Jerusalem, and you King Jehoshaphat. The Lord says this to you: Be not afraid or dismayed at this great multitude; for the battle is not yours, but God's.

I find it interesting that the Spirit of the Lord didn't come upon Jehoshaphat. It came upon one of the believers in the midst of the congregation. God doesn't always use the most likely candidate. He often uses the unusual and the unlikely, so He alone gets all the glory for the outcome.

What was the message the Spirit of God gave them that day? Was it one of defeat and discouragement? Did He tell them they were doomed? No! He encouraged them and assured them that He was with them. Just knowing you are not alone and that God has not forgotten about you can breathe strength and courage into your weary soul! Let's continue reading the next few verses:

2 CHRONICLES 20:16-17 (Amplified)

16 Tomorrow go down to them. Behold, they will come up by the Ascent of Ziz, and you will find them at the end of the ravine before the Wilderness of Jeruel.

17 You shall not need to fight in this battle; take your positions, stand still, and see the deliverance of the Lord [Who is] with you, O Judah and Jerusalem. Fear not nor be dismayed. Tomorrow go out against them, for the Lord is with you.

Notice how the Lord didn't deny the fact that a great multitude was coming against them. He didn't say, "What army? I don't see an army. You need to walk by faith and not by sight. Just ignore all of those soldiers and they will disappear!"

Real Bible faith doesn't ignore the issues or deny the existence of challenges; instead, faith declares the answer and magnifies God and the Word above the problem. Faith refuses to be afraid of the big, bad devil and all of his threats. When you are in faith, you know that you know that God is going to see you through *in style!*

The Spirit of the Lord reminded the people not to get into fear, but to stay in faith and trust. The last part of the word of the Lord that day was awesome—". . . *the battle is not yours, but God's*" (2 Chron. 20:15 Amplified).

The Lord takes it personally when His people are attacked. Remember the Apostle Paul's conversion? (See Acts chapter 9.) While he was on the road to Damascus, a light from Heaven shone upon him and he heard a voice from Heaven say, "Saul, why are you persecuting Me?" Saul was killing and persecuting the Christians, but Jesus took it extremely personally.

It is no different in our lives today. Doesn't the Bible say we are one with the Lord? We are in Him and He is in us. (See John 15:1–8.) When we are attacked by the enemy or people who are influenced by wrong spirits, God sees it as an attack against Him. I guess that pretty much assures us of victory!

The Lord said the battle was His, but notice that He also told them to do something. *"Tomorrow go out against them, for the Lord is with you"* (2 Chron. 20:17 Amplified). God has His part, but we also have ours, which always involves trusting and obeying.

The people had to get up and face the enemy. They wouldn't have won the victory if their attitude was, "God said the battle was His, so I am sleeping in. I am staying right here in my cozy tent." No! They had to act upon all that the Lord had said, and He had said, "Go face the enemy."

Send Out the Praise Team

The next verses tell us even more about how they faced this battle:

2 CHRONICLES 20:20–22 (Amplified)

20 And they rose early in the morning and went out into the Wilderness of Tekoa; and as they went out, Jehoshaphat

stood and said, Hear me, O Judah, and you inhabitants of Jerusalem! Believe in the Lord your God and you shall be established; believe and remain steadfast to His prophets and you shall prosper.

21 When he had consulted with the people, he appointed singers to sing to the Lord and praise Him in their holy [priestly] garments as they went out before the army, saying, Give thanks to the Lord, for His mercy and loving-kindness endure forever!

22 And when they began to sing and to praise, the Lord set ambushments against the men of Ammon, Moab, and Mount Seir who had come against Judah, and they were [self-] slaughtered.

I am not sure exactly when the Lord revealed the next step to Jehoshaphat. It was probably during the night while everyone else was sound asleep. The people woke up refreshed and excited. They may have still been on a spiritual high from the day before. "Whooo-hooo! We've got a plan from God. Oh, what a great day this is going to be!"

Jehoshaphat had a revelation concerning the rest of the story, but I like the way he eased into it. He started by reminding them of what had happened the day before. "Remember our word from God? You believed His word. You received His word."

They replied, "Oh yes, Jehoshaphat, we are tracking with you. God has our back!"

Then Jehoshaphat continued by saying, "How many worshippers and singers do we have in the crowd?" If that group of people was anything like most churches today, I am sure multitudes were rushing to the front of the crowd, vying for a spot on the praise team. They were probably anxious to finally get the opportunity to display the talents that, up to this point, had failed to be acknowledged or recognized!

As the singers began to gather, their mission and assignment were revealed. "You're going to go out first—in front of the army. You're going to be the ones the Ammonites, the Moabites, and all the other enemies see first. And you're not going to have a sword or spear. You're going to have a tambourine."

"What?" they must have exclaimed. "Wait just a minute. I misunderstood. I can't really sing. You want me to prove it? I can't really carry a tune, Jehoshaphat. I think I'd better move out of the way so the real singers can come forward. I-I-I just lost my song."

How many of you would have liked to have been in the choir that day? It didn't make much sense in the natural to send out the praise team instead of soldiers. But God's thoughts and ways are higher than ours. The victory was theirs, and it was not won through any natural means. It was brought about through prayer, seeking the Lord, and praising God.

As they walked out toward those vast armies, they began to say, "'*Praise the Lord, For His mercy endures forever*'" (v. 21). I'm sure when they first began to say those words, it was a little bit weak, and their knees were probably knocking together while their voices were shaking. But the more they said it, the stronger the praise became. It welled up on the inside of them, and they began to believe what they were saying. "Praise the Lord, for His mercy endures forever!" The Lord intervened and their enemies killed each other before Judah even reached the enemy camp. They were all slain.

2 CHRONICLES 20:23-24

23 For the people of Ammon and Moab stood up against the inhabitants of Mount Seir to utterly kill and destroy them. And when they had made an end of the inhabitants of Seir, they helped to destroy one another.

24 So when Judah came to a place overlooking the wilderness, they looked toward the multitude; and there were their dead bodies, fallen on the earth. No one had escaped.

What a victory! What a supernatural deliverance! What divine intervention was wrought that day! But the defeat of their enemies was not the end of the story. Winning the battle would have been great. Just not being killed would have been wonderful. But God said, "Because you prayed, because you obeyed, because you praised Me when things didn't look good in the natural, I am going to do exceedingly, abundantly above what you were expecting Me to do in this situation."

The last part of Second Chronicles 20:20 gives us the key to what God had in mind, " *'Believe in the Lord your God, and you shall be established; believe His prophets, and you shall prosper.'* " God didn't just want them to escape death. He wanted them to come out of this situation better off than they were when it started. I have stated this previously, but I must repeat it: "God will restore and make better than before."

When the enemy comes to steal, kill, and destroy, God intends to make him pay! He knew all of those armies were going to gather against His people, but He told them not to be afraid. He urged them to believe in Him and believe the word of the Lord from His prophets, and they would *prosper*! That is exactly what happened:

2 CHRONICLES 20:25

25 When Jehoshaphat and his people came to take away their spoil, they found among them an abundance of valuables on the dead bodies, and precious jewelry, which they stripped off for themselves, more than they could carry away; and they were three days gathering the spoil because there was so much.

God has ways and means to get things to us that we have not even imagined. There was more than one miracle that happened on that particular day. Certainly it was a miracle that all of those enemy soldiers ended up dead. But it was also divine intervention that they wore their jewels into battle. How dumb is that? Angels must have been in the tents that day, saying to those soldiers, "You know, that gold chain would really look good with that outfit you're wearing. Oh my, those ruby earrings are stunning. And don't forget to wear that emerald ring! Get your 'bling' on. You want them to see you coming!"

Just think how supernatural the whole event was. It was definitely divine intervention. The Bible does not say the children of Israel had to go into the enemies' tents and find their treasures. It says they stripped them off their dead bodies. Their enemies wore their valuables into battle. That tells me that God knows how to get things to us!

Don't be concerned about the "how." You're hooked up with the "Who." Just praise Him. Magnify Him. Offer up to Him power-packed prayers, accompanied with heartfelt praise.

Do you remember the phrase in verse 25—"*more than they could carry away*"? It took the children of Israel three days to gather up the spoils. That was an amazing slap in the face of their enemies. All of their wealth was now going to be used to support God's people! What the devil meant for harm and destruction, God turned around and received glory from. That is what God has planned for your life!

The next time you find yourself in a position where you are being bombarded on every side and loss and defeat seem to be inevitable, remember this powerful statement I heard Rev. Kenneth E. Hagin say years ago: "Prayer plus praise equals more than you can carry away!"

CHAPTER 11

Cheer Up!

I love this story I once heard about a parakeet named Chippie. Perhaps you can relate. The bird's problems began when his owner decided to clean up the seeds and loose feathers from the bottom of his cage by using her vacuum cleaner. When the phone rang the owner turned to pick it up, and you guessed it, with a thud and a swoosh, Chippie was gone.

The owner quickly turned off the vacuum and unzipped the bag. There was Chippie—stunned but still breathing. Seeing that he was covered with black dust, his owner rushed Chippie to the bathtub where she turned on the faucet full blast and held the bird under the icy water. At that point, she realized that she had done even more damage to the poor bird. She quickly cranked up her blow dryer and gave the wet, shivering little parakeet an overly powerful blast. The story ends, "Chippie doesn't sing much any more."

Do you get the point? Chippie had a rough day. Chippie lost his will to sing. He lost his joy. Too many of God's people don't sing anymore. They've lost their will to sing. They've lost their joy. But God wants to restore it!

You may be knocked down but you're not knocked out! Get up, and get up with a song in your heart. Don't let a bad day, a weird week, a terrible month, or even an awful year steal your joy and rob you of the song Jesus wants to put in your heart.

When we are facing a difficult situation, one of the first things we are tempted to do is lose our joy. Nehemiah 8:10 says, *"Then he said to them, 'Go your way, eat the fat, drink the sweet, and send portions to those for whom nothing is prepared; for this day is holy to our Lord. Do not sorrow, for the joy of the Lord is your strength.'"* If our joy is drained, so is our strength. When we become weak, it is difficult to fight the good fight of faith.

Joy is a spiritual force and must be evident in our lives as believers if we are to overcome and walk in victory in every situation of life. Jesus was very aware of this powerful force. On numerous occasions, He instructed His followers to "be of good cheer."

When He ran into people who were full of agony and despair, He wasn't like the guy walking across a bridge who saw another man about to jump. The first man went over and tried to stop him. He asked, "What's going on in your life?" The fellow who wanted to jump started telling him all the terrible issues which had gotten him to that point. What the first man heard was so bad that he grabbed the other man's hand and said, "I'll jump with you. Let's just end it all right now."

No, whenever Jesus shows up, He has a good report. In this chapter, we'll look at four occasions when Jesus told people to "be of good cheer." He told them to do that when dealing with sin and sickness and when facing fear, persecution, and tribulation.

Every time Jesus told somebody to "be of good cheer," the last thing that person wanted to do was be happy, do a little dance, or be full of joy. But Jesus is the One Who brings joy.

Jesus is the original author of cheer. He wants His people to cheer up! The word *cheer* means "to bring encouragement, to give courage to, to put in good spirits, and to provide happiness or joy."

How can we cheer up and be glad, no matter what we are going through? We can do that because Jesus is the answer. Nothing is too difficult for Him.

There's no pit too deep or problem too big that Jesus isn't able to get you out of it or bring you the answer you need. That's why you can cheer up. That's why Jesus told people to "be of good cheer" when He walked into a situation.

When someone's relative was dying or someone was in prison, He would say, "Be of good cheer." He was really saying, "Your answer has come. Your problem is solved. You've got a reason now to brighten up and put a smile on your face."

When He said, "Be of good cheer," He was saying, "Gird up the loins of your mind. Take courage. It isn't going to end like this." Jesus put into operation the first definition of the word *cheer*. Wherever He went, He brought *encouragement*.

Another meaning of *cheer* is "to put in good spirits." Some people just carry a good attitude around with them. They have a good spirit. You might be having a down day, but when you get around a person who is singing, rejoicing, and happy in Jesus, it gets on you! When Jesus showed up, He automatically put people in good spirits because He had a good spirit about Him.

The last meaning of *cheer* is "to provide happiness or joy." Jesus went about spreading good cheer and encouragement. He gave people courage and restored their joy.

The first place Jesus said, "Be of good cheer" was in the face of sin and sickness. Have you ever faced a sickness or disease? Have you ever been bound by sin? Well, we all were before we found Jesus. But in the face of sickness and sin, Jesus said, "Be of good cheer."

MATTHEW 9:1–8

1 So He got into a boat, crossed over, and came to His own city.

2 Then behold, they brought to Him a paralytic lying on a bed. When Jesus saw their faith, He said to the paralytic, "Son, be of good cheer; your sins are forgiven you."

3 And at once some of the scribes said within themselves, "This Man blasphemes!"

4 But Jesus, knowing their thoughts, said, "Why do you think evil in your hearts?

5 For which is easier, to say, 'Your sins are forgiven you,' or to say, 'Arise and walk'?

6 But that you may know that the Son of Man has power on earth to forgive sins"—then He said to the paralytic, "Arise, take up your bed, and go to your house."

7 And he arose and departed to his house.

8 Now when the multitudes saw it, they marveled and glorified God, who had given such power to men.

This man needed healing, but it's interesting to me that the first thing Jesus said to him was, "Son, be of good cheer; your sins are forgiven you." Maybe this paralyzed man had been around a bunch of religious people who told him, "Oh, you've got the palsy because of some deep, dark sin." Religious people don't give you good, cheery news. Most of the time they only have bad news.

One time Jesus and His disciples came upon a man born blind. The disciples asked, *"Who sinned, this man or his parents, that he was born blind?"* (John 9:2). And Jesus said, *"Neither . . ."* (v. 3).

Notice that sickness isn't always a result of sin. But Jesus' telling the paralytic "Your sins are forgiven you" says to me that someone had told him he was a filthy, rotten sinner who was sick because of his sin. So Jesus wanted to set the record straight. He told the man, "Hey, I didn't borrow this sickness from the devil and put it on you. I didn't bring this sickness on you to teach you a lesson." He wanted this man to know that even if he had sinned, God wasn't holding his past sins and failures against him. This man wasn't being punished for something he did 20 years ago.

The devil still tries to use this tactic on us today. Sometimes he uses men and women behind pulpits to heap condemnation on people and say that some bad thing happened to them because they committed some terrible sin. Some horrible disease came upon them because when they were children they were sassy to their parents. Satan tries to dig up all the garbage from our past and use it against us so we won't rise up and resist negative thoughts. But our past sins and failures are *none of his business!* Once we confess them and ask for forgiveness, they are under the blood!

Jesus was saying to the paralytic and He's saying to us today: "Be of good cheer! Be lifted! Be encouraged! Your past cannot hold you in bondage any longer. You've got to let it go. Be of good cheer. Your sins are forgiven. Be of good cheer. Whatever you did, however you failed, it's under the blood."

Remember, Psalm 103:12 says, *"As far as the east is from the west, So far has He removed our transgressions from us."*

When wrong thoughts try to trouble you, begin to declare out loud, "No, I don't receive that. My heart is clean and clear. I have forgiven everyone who has wronged me in the past, and thank God, I am forgiven."

Be of good cheer. Your sins are forgiven. Be of good cheer. *"There is therefore now no condemnation to those who are in Christ Jesus"* (Rom. 8:1). Don't receive the devil's condemnation. If you have repented, know this: The blood of Jesus is a cleansing agent. It is a forgiving agent. There is no sin that we could ever commit that the blood of Jesus cannot cleanse us of. If we hold on to things from our past, we are saying that those things are too big for the blood to take care of.

Friend, there is nothing too big for the blood. Jesus looked at that paralytic and said, "Son, be of good cheer; your sins are forgiven you." If you are holding on to something from your past that you have repented of, then the Lord is saying to you right now, just as He said to the paralytic, "Let it go. Be of good cheer." Jesus was saying to that man, "Be of good cheer. There's a Healer in the house."

Acts 10:38 hadn't been written yet. But if it had been, Jesus might have quoted it about Himself: *"How God anointed Jesus of Nazareth with the Holy Spirit and with power, who went about doing good and healing all who were oppressed by the devil, for God was with Him."* Does it say that Jesus went about doing bad? No! He went about doing good!

Be of good cheer! You are healed in the Name of Jesus. Be of good cheer! God has anointed the Lord to set the captives free. Be of good cheer! God has brought deliverance to those who were oppressed. Sickness and disease are oppressions, and if the devil has tried to attack you physically, start saying, "I'm the redeemed. I'm healed. I'm whole. I'm going to be of good cheer, because Jesus bore my sicknesses and carried my pains. I receive strength, health, and quickening. I'm of good cheer because I don't have to be bound by sickness and disease."

Friend, it's good news for the sick when they find out they don't have to be sick anymore! It was good news for me when I found out that Jesus took those stripes upon His back for my healing.

You're redeemed from the curse of sickness and death. You're not under that curse anymore. That ought to make you happy. You ought to cheer up and be encouraged! You ought to be joyful because of what Jesus has done for you. Everything you need in every area of your life has been abundantly provided for in the Lord!

Be of Good Cheer in the Face of Fear

Secondly, Jesus said to be of good cheer in the face of fear. We see an example of this in Matthew chapter 14, which we discussed in a previous chapter. This passage begins with the account of Herod the Tetrarch beheading John the Baptist. When Jesus heard the news, he departed by ship to a deserted place. Thousands of people followed Him on foot, and when He saw them, He had compassion on them and healed their sick. Then He fed them supernaturally—5,000 men plus the women and children. That was a big crowd, and His disciples witnessed this awesome miracle.

As this long day came to a close, Jesus told His disciples to get into the ship and go to the other side. Then He sent the multitude away and went up onto the mountain by Himself to pray. In a way He was saying, "I need some alone time."

Have you ever had a big, full, busy day and all you wanted to do was get into bed with "me, myself, and I" and have some alone time with Jesus? Well, He was saying, "I need some alone time with the Father. You guys go on ahead to the other side."

While Jesus was praying, His disciples "hit a snag." Do you know what that means? Hitting a snag means you're going along just fine and suddenly you bump into something that you can't get through, over, or around. A friend of ours told us a great story about a banjo player on the old *Hee Haw* television show that illustrates what it means to "hit a snag." This banjo player was still performing well up into his eighties. During a show, he stopped playing, looked at those around him and said, "Boys, I have hit a snag," and fell over dead!

Jesus' disciples weren't dead, but out there on that ship, they got into trouble. They hit a snag. The devil was angry about all the miracles that had happened that day. I'm sure he schemed up a plan and thought, "I'm going to devise a way to kill them. Jesus isn't here, and He's the One with all the power. I'm going to devise a way to take out His entire evangelistic team in one quick sweep."

You know, that's what the devil wanted. It's what he would have liked to do. The wind was boisterous. The devil was out there blowing on the waves and creating a big stir. I'm sure he was laughing and saying to himself, "Look how scared they are. These boys are really afraid, and Jesus isn't here to save them." The devil wanted to fill the disciples with fear. He had this whole plot schemed up, but it didn't work, even though Jesus wasn't there!

Jesus was a Man of prayer, and He was in the Spirit. He knew immediately that His disciples were in trouble. The Spirit of God showed Him, and He came to their rescue. The Holy Spirit didn't show Jesus what was happening to His disciples so He could sit by and do nothing. He showed Jesus so He could help them.

If you'll be a person of prayer, even if your kids are off course or in the midst of a storm, God's Spirit will show you when they're in trouble. And He'll do it so you can do something about it—through your prayers. When the Holy Spirit gives you a warning on the inside that some of your relatives are in danger, it's so you can pray for God to make a way of escape to keep them from being hurt. That's what Jesus did for His disciples.

Jesus prayed, and as He did, not only did He see that they were in trouble, but He went to where they were. And He'll do the same thing for you and your loved ones. He'll go to where you are and minister to you.

We pick up Matthew's account of this incident as Jesus was going to help His troubled disciples.

MATTHEW 14:25-32

25 Now in the fourth watch of the night Jesus went to them, walking on the sea.

26 And when the disciples saw Him walking on the sea, they were troubled, saying, "It is a ghost!" And they cried out for fear.

27 But immediately Jesus spoke to them, saying, "Be of good cheer! It is I; do not be afraid."

28 And Peter answered Him and said, "Lord, if it is You, command me to come to You on the water."

29 So He said, "Come." And when Peter had come down out of the boat, he walked on the water to go to Jesus.

30 But when he saw that the wind was boisterous, he was afraid; and beginning to sink he cried out, saying, "Lord, save me!"

31 And immediately Jesus stretched out His hand and caught him, and said to him, "O you of little faith, why did you doubt?"

32 And when they got into the boat, the wind ceased.

There are so many things in this story we could focus on, but we're just going to highlight some of them. First of all, notice that the disciples were afraid of the storm, but they were more afraid of Jesus. "It's a ghost!" they cried. Isn't that something? People immediately think that the devil has more supernatural power than Jesus.

But what were Jesus' first words? "Be of good cheer. It is I. Be not afraid." Peter got out of the boat and walked to the Lord based on one word—"Come." I think it's kind of comical that as Peter was walking on the water, he heard the wind howling, saw the waves crashing, and started thinking, *Oh, I can't walk on this water. It's really stormy.* If it had been a clear, still day, would it have been any easier for him to walk on the water?

But he started listening to all the junk. The devil was screaming in his ear and trying to bring fear—stirring up the waves, splashing water in his face, and getting the wind to blow his hair around. All of these circumstances caused fear to come into Peter's heart. But Jesus was saying to him and He's saying to us today, "Don't be afraid to step out on My Word."

Peter had one word, "Come." We have the full Word of God—66 books of the Bible. We have revelation knowledge. And Jesus is saying to us, "Be of good cheer. Don't be afraid to step out on My Word. Don't let fear hold you back."

Do you have some goals? Do you have some dreams? Do you have some things you want to reach for? Don't let fear prevent you from reaching your goals. Be like Peter. Get out of the boat and walk on top of your fear. Be of good cheer!

We have nothing to be afraid of. Jesus is with us. He's in us. He's for us. He said, "*'I will never leave you nor forsake you'*" (Heb. 13:5). Jesus is the Master over any kind of fear that would try to come against us. We need to "be of good cheer" instead of being full of fear. The things that we're believing for are going to come to pass if we'll walk in the Word of God and stand on His promises. I'll say it again. Be of good cheer! Don't be full of fear!

Be of Good Cheer When Persecution Comes

The third area where Jesus said for us to "be of good cheer" is in the face of persecution. Have you ever had an opportunity to be persecuted? Acts chapters 21 and 22 contain the account of Paul preaching in Jerusalem. The Sanhedrin and the Pharisees were all stirred up over what Paul was preaching, and they couldn't decide whether or not to believe him. The religious people were so agitated and there was so much turmoil in the city that the Roman officials actually arrested Paul for his own safety. They thought the people were going to tear his limbs off, so they took him into custody.

Isn't that something? Paul was doing the will of God—preaching the Gospel—and yet he was being persecuted.

Sometimes we can be smack-dab in the middle of the perfect will of God, but persecution still comes. Jesus always has a word of encouragement for us in the midst of it all. He had a word for Paul in that jail cell. The Bible says in Acts 23:11, *"But the following night the Lord stood by him and said, 'Be of good cheer, Paul; for as you have testified for Me in Jerusalem, so you must also bear witness at Rome.'"*

Notice that Jesus didn't send an angel. He came Himself. The Lord stood by Paul and told him, "Be of good cheer." What was He saying? He was saying, "Paul, I'm bringing you encouragement. I'm bringing you courage. I'm bringing you what you need to finish your course."

Can you draw encouragement from the fact that the Lord stood by Paul? This was a dark time for him. This was a difficult season. Suddenly he was sitting there in prison, thinking, *What now? Here I am giving the sermon of my life and look where it got me.*

He might have been tempted to feel sorry for himself. He was probably feeling a little bit down when, all of a sudden, the Lord was standing by him. Friend, the Lord is with us, in us, and for us. But it's encouraging to know that when we need Him, He's standing by us.

Jesus is surrounding us. He's undergirding us. He's standing there as our guard. He's standing there as our defense, our refuge, and our strength.

You might feel as if you're about to collapse under the pressures of life. But know this—Jesus is standing right behind you. He has His arms outstretched and He's upholding you. There's nothing that can knock Jesus down. There's nothing that can make Him fall, and guess what? You're not going to fall either. No matter what lies are spoken, no matter what people say in a time of persecution, you can "be of good cheer" because the Lord is standing with you.

It's good to have good praying partners. It's good to have faith buddies—I love them! But even if you can't get in touch with anyone else, you can always call on the Lord. Jeremiah 33:3 is His phone number—" *'Call to Me, and I will answer you, and show you great and mighty things, which you do not know.'* " The Lord will stand with you. The Lord will come into agreement with you. The Lord will uphold you, even the Lord Jesus Christ.

I think Paul might have gotten happy when he looked up and saw the Lord standing there. That would have been enough to make me say, "Okay, I'm all better now. I'm not in this jail cell alone. I'm not in this dark place by myself. Jesus is here with me." And it wasn't the first time Jesus showed up in a difficult situation.

Remember Shadrach, Meshach, and Abednego? What happened when they were in that fiery furnace? The furnace was so hot that it killed the men who threw them into the fire. And yet they weren't burned or even singed. The king declared, "Didn't we throw three men into the fire? But I see four men now, and the Fourth Man is like the Son of God." (See Dan. 3:24–25.) How did he know that? He didn't say the Fourth Man was an angel. He said, "He's the Son of God."

No matter how hot the heat, no matter how difficult the situation, no matter how mean the persecution, the Fourth Man is standing with you. The Fourth Man is surrounding you and giving you strength. That makes me happy just reading about it. I don't know if Paul got that happy, but I'm happy for him because Jesus showed up in his jail cell!

Think about all the ordeals the Apostle Paul had to face. He was stoned, shipwrecked, and beaten, but none of those things mattered to him when Jesus showed up. Jesus stood by him through it all. I'm telling you, that's a good word. The Lord Jesus stood by him and this is what He said: "Be of good cheer, Paul." He knew Paul by name. He didn't show up and say, "Be of good cheer. Now, what was your name?" The Lord knows us by name! He knows what we're going through.

Then Jesus said to Paul, "You've done what I told you to do in Jerusalem, and you're going to finish what I've told you to do. You must go to Rome, and there isn't any persecution, religious spirit, or crazy devil that can stop the will, plan, and purpose of God from coming to pass in your life."

The devil threw all kinds of attacks at Paul, but he finished his course. He did what Jesus told him to do. And this is what Paul said—"*But none of these things move me, neither count I my life dear unto myself, so that I might finish my course with joy*" (Acts 20:24 KJV).

We're not going to halfway finish. We're not going to have Jesus say to us, "Well?" And we're not going to have Him say, "Undone." We're going to hear the Lord say to us, " '*Well done, good and faithful servant*' " (Matt. 25:23).

That's what Paul was aiming for. He said, "I don't count my life dear unto myself, so that I might finish my course with joy." How did he say he was going to finish his course? Did he say he was going to be worn out and burned out when he finished? No! He said he was going to finish his course with joy.

In Second Timothy 4:7 Paul also said, "*I have fought a good fight, I have finished my course, I have kept the faith*" (KJV). That ought to be our testimony, no matter what the devil says he's going to do or how much turmoil he stirs up. We are not going to quit, we are not going to fear, and we are not going to back down in the face of persecution. We are not going to lose our joy. We are going to finish all that God has called us to do!

Be of Good Cheer in the Face of Tribulation

The fourth area where Jesus said for us to be of good cheer was in the face of tribulation. John 16:33 in *The Amplified Bible* says: "*I have told you these things, so that in Me you may have [perfect] peace and confidence. In the world you have tribulation and trials and distress and frustration;* [Note: We don't need to center on that; we've all been there and done that.] *but be of good cheer [take courage; be confident, certain, undaunted]! For I have overcome the world. [I have deprived it of power to harm you and have conquered it for you.]*"

Jesus realized that in the world we are going to have tribulation, distress, and frustration, but we're not centering on that. Immediately He gave His disciples a solution for it all. It was the words—"Be of good cheer."

Why, Lord? Why can we be of good cheer? Because He has overcome the world. He has taken away its power to harm us. He has deprived it of that power.

He was telling the disciples, "Don't be concerned about all of this stuff that's going on in the world. Be of good cheer. I've overcome the world." He was saying, "*Greater is he that is in you, than he that is in the world"* (1 John 4:4 KJV). Take courage! Be encouraged! Cheer up! Rejoice!

Jesus wants us to know that there's a secret weapon to help us overcome the world and the tactics of the enemy. What's that secret weapon, Jesus? Rejoice! "Be of good cheer." *"Rejoice in the Lord always. Again I will say, rejoice!"* (Phil. 4:4). Don't rejoice because of the temptations, trials, tribulations, or persecutions. Rejoice because Jesus has already overcome them all. "Rejoice in Me," says the Lord.

Rejoicing is a demonstration of our faith in God. Being of good cheer shows that we believe the Word of God is true. Christians ought to be the happiest people on earth. We ought to be full of good cheer because Jesus has given us victory in every single area of life. If we don't rejoice when all the attacks are coming against us, the devil will think he is winning. But if we act on the Word regardless of the situation, we are making a statement that we believe God is working on our behalf, no matter what. And we WIN!

All the times that Jesus said, "Be of good cheer," He was really saying the same thing that James said in James 1:2–4: *"My brethren, count it all joy when you fall into various trials, knowing that the testing of your faith produces patience. But let patience have its perfect work, that you may be perfect and complete, lacking nothing."*

When we rejoice in the Lord, when we cheer up, and when we act on the Word of God, we're going to come out lacking nothing. Jesus knew the value of releasing the force of joy in our lives. In the remainder of this book, let's look in detail at this powerful spiritual force.

CHAPTER 12

The Restorative Power of Joy

As I said in the previous chapter, joy is a spiritual force. It is not based on our external situations or circumstances. All hell can be breaking loose in our lives, but when we know how to tap into the force of joy we will remain steadfast and immovable because our eyes are on Jesus and the promises in His Word. That gives us confidence about the way things will turn out. We win!

I like this definition of *joy*: "the inner passion excited by the expectation of *good*"! Are you expecting God to intervene in your life and circumstances? If you are, then you are expecting *good* to show up because God is good. When He comes on the scene, something good is going to happen to you!

Did you know there is power in joy to restore—to get back what the enemy has tried to steal from us? You can't beat a joyful believer! And when you rejoice in the Lord your God, you're going to get everything back.

I heard a minister several years ago say, "If Satan can't steal your joy, he can't keep your goods."[9] The devil may have tried to steal some things from you, but he can't keep them if you will rise up and act on the Word of God and declare, "Restore!"

Too often we are waiting until we see something happen in the natural before we are filled with joy. We're waiting until we have a confirmation that things have changed. But that isn't biblical joy. That is happiness, and there is a difference.

Happiness is a feeling that is based on situations and circumstances. Happiness says, "I'll be happy when the bills are all paid, my husband is nice, the kids get all A's, and the dog obeys." It's all based on what is going on around us and life being wonderful and everything great. But we can still have joy even when the bills aren't paid, the husband isn't nice, and the kids don't get all A's. We can still have joy because it's an inner force. It comes from the inside and it stems from who we are, Whose we are, and what we know.

Do you know in Whom you have believed, and are you fully persuaded that He is able and willing to keep that which you have committed unto Him (2 Tim. 1:12)? Are you fully persuaded that He is the Author and Finisher of your faith (Heb. 12:2)? Are you fully persuaded that He that has begun a good work in you will perform it until the day of Jesus Christ (Phil. 1:6)?

It's not over until it's over. We don't play nine-inning games. We play until we win. As I've said before, it's our bat, it's our ball, and our Father is the umpire. He's calling the shots. So don't lose hope. Don't give up and don't quit. Keep rejoicing in the midst of whatever you may be facing.

The Bible tells us to rejoice at odd times. It doesn't tell us to rejoice when everything is going great. It tells us to rejoice when we fall into diverse temptations (James 1:2 KJV). All hell can be breaking loose around us, but the force of joy will sustain us. It will steady us and keep us on course. It will also strengthen us. It will give us the power to get up and get out of anything that the devil tries to throw our way.

Let's take a closer look at James 1:2–4, *"My brethren, count it all joy when you fall into various trials, knowing that the testing of your faith produces patience. But let patience have its perfect work, that you may be perfect and complete, lacking nothing."*

"My brethren, count it all *joy*. . . ." That's got to be a misprint. It should say, "Count it all *sorrow* when you fall into various trials." Or how about, "Count it all *unfair* when you fall into various trials? Count it all, 'Why, God, why? Why is this happening to me? I'm a good person. I'm a giver. I'm walking in love. Why? Why? Why?' " Whine, whine, whine.

Is that what it says? No. It says, "Count it all *joy* when you fall into various trials." Notice it doesn't say when you fall into one trial. It says when you fall into various trials. That means more than one at the same time. It means that the washing machine might stop working, the car might break down, the air conditioning system might quit, you might lose your job, you might get attacked with the flu, and it might all happen at the same time.

That isn't fair. That doesn't seem right. But the Bible says that we are to count it all joy when we fall into various trials all at the same time. What enables us to do that? The answer is found in verse 3—". . . *knowing that the testing of your faith produces patience.*"

We are able to count it all joy because of what we know—knowing that the Word of God is true, knowing that we have a covenant with a covenant-keeping God, knowing that Jesus has redeemed us from the curse of the law, and knowing that God hasn't fallen off the throne just because we can't pay our house payment.

What else do we know? We know that the Word of God says He supplies all of our needs according to His riches in glory by Christ Jesus (Phil. 4:19). We know that if we are tithers, we have resources stored up for us in Heaven. If we have given, it will be given unto us, good measure, pressed down, shaken together, and running over (Luke 6:38).

When we know these things, if temptation comes in the financial realm, we know that we have every right to draw from our heavenly bank account to meet our need (Phil. 4:17). We know that the Bible says the windows of Heaven are open unto the tither (Mal. 3:10). That's why we can count it all joy when the checkbook may not say what it needs to say.

We can also count it all joy when sickness and disease try to attack our bodies, because we know that by Jesus' stripes we are healed (Isa. 53:5). Himself (Jesus) took our infirmities and bore our sicknesses (Matt. 8:17). We "know that we know that we know" that anything in this natural world is subject to change. It is subject to the unchangeable Word of the Living God!

Even though these things may be swirling all around us, we can lift up our hands by faith and begin to rejoice. We're not thanking God for the tests and trials because He didn't send them. But we are thanking Him for the way out. We are thanking Him that *"No temptation has overtaken you except such as is common to man; but God is faithful, who will not allow you to be tempted beyond what you are able, but with the temptation will also make the way of escape, that you may be able to bear it"* (1 Cor. 10:13).

We will all be able to get to a safe landing place if we'll just do what the Word says. And we're not going to come through our trials just barely hanging on. We're not going to come through with our hair singed by fire and our acrylic nails melted by the heat.

No, we're going to come through each and every trial without the smell of smoke on us. That's what our God does for us. He gets us safely to the other side!

We can rejoice in the midst of the trials because we know *something* and *Somebody.* We know in Whom we have believed and are fully persuaded that He is able to deliver us. We know Him through the Word and through our past experiences. We don't base our Christian life on experiences, but when we experience victory, it encourages our faith.

I like what a little lady had written in her Bible. A minister was looking through her Bible, and next to all of these scriptures she had written the letters TP. So he inquired, "What does that mean?"

And she replied, "Tried and proven."

Do you have any TPs written in your Bible?

Our God is a Master at fixing any disaster. When we call on His Name, and all of our hope, faith, trust, and confidence is in Him, we can begin to boldly declare, "My God is bigger than any problem. He's bigger than any mountain. I'm a winner. I'm more than a conqueror. I don't care what the devil says. It's going to go God's way."

Did you know that God has ways, means, avenues, angels, and even divine, supernatural intervention, if necessary, to get you out of that mess? It may even be a mess that you created yourself. But His mercy endures forever, and He's still the Master at fixing any disaster. That should give you plenty of reasons to rejoice!

Rejoicing Brings God on the Scene

I love the Lord and I love the way He operates. He just does things supernaturally. He does things beyond our wildest imagination. Our attitude when we are facing difficult situations determines our altitude. If we're whining, complaining, and murmuring, it won't get us very far. Just ask the children of Israel—that was what got them into trouble. But rejoicing always brings God on the scene.

We can learn a valuable lesson from a guy in the Bible who was going through a really tough time. Talk about various trials! Just read what this man was experiencing. *"Though the fig tree may not blossom, Nor fruit be on the vines; Though the labor of the olive may fail, And the fields yield no food; Though the flock may be cut off from the fold, And there be no herd in the stalls . . ."* (Hab. 3:17).

That sounds like bad news, doesn't it? That sounds like a terrible day. There are trials with the fig trees and trials with the flock. There are trials in the fields. Every area of this man's livelihood is being attacked.

What did he do? Look at verses 18 and 19, *"Yet I will rejoice in the Lord, I will joy in the God of my salvation. The Lord God is my strength; He will make my feet like deer's feet, And He will make me walk on my high hills."* What was he doing? First of all, he made the decision to rejoice. And how did he rejoice? He began to magnify the Lord. He began to declare some things. He said, "The Lord is my strength. The Lord will make my feet like hinds' feet" (v. 19 KJV).

The hind is a red-tailed deer, and I'm told that you can hardly fence these animals in. They can leap high fences. So what was Habakkuk saying? "Devil, you can't fence me in.

136

There might be a test here, a trial there, some trouble here, and some lack there. But my God is coming upon me. He's anointing my feet, and I'm going to leap right out of this mess. You can't fence me in!" That's what he was saying. There is always a way out with God.

In this passage, the word *joy* is not some kind of quiet, inner strength. According to *Strong's Concordance* it means to be glad, to be joyful, and it suggests dancing and leaping for joy. The verb originally meant to spin around with intense emotion.[10]

This is contrary to the idea that the biblical concept of joy is only an inner sense of well being. That's well and good, but there comes a time when you have to act upon the Word of God. There comes a time when you have to lift your hands. You have to shout unto the Lord. You may even need to dance or spin around. You have to do whatever it takes to release the joy of the Lord on the inside of you and shake off depression and oppression.

There's restorative power in joy. Joy will restore and it will make things better than before. God doesn't just give back what the enemy stole. He gives all of that back plus even more, added and multiplied unto you. You can't beat a joyful believer!

I want to look at a passage of scripture in the Book of Joel:

JOEL 2:21–27

21 Fear not, O land; Be glad and rejoice, For the Lord has done marvelous things!

22 Do not be afraid, you beasts of the field; For the open pastures are springing up, And the tree bears its fruit; The fig tree and the vine yield their strength.

23 Be glad then, you children of Zion, And rejoice in the Lord your God; For He has given you the former rain faithfully, And He will cause the rain to come down for you—The former rain, And the latter rain in the first month.

24 The threshing floors shall be full of wheat, And the vats shall overflow with new wine and oil.

25 "So I will restore to you the years that the swarming locust has eaten, The crawling locust, The consuming locust, And the chewing locust, My great army which I sent among you.

26 You shall eat in plenty and be satisfied, And praise the name of the Lord your God, Who has dealt wondrously with you; And My people shall never be put to shame.

27 Then you shall know that I am in the midst of Israel: I am the Lord your God And there is no other. My people shall never be put to shame."

What are our instructions for receiving restoration? We find three things listed in verse 21:

1. Fear not.

2. Be glad.

3. Rejoice.

The first thing we have to do is fear not. If we're going to operate in restoration we cannot fear. Fear connects us to the things that we don't desire. But we have been given the ability to resist fear and put it out of our lives. We need to be "Teflon® Christians." That means nothing sticks to us. Whatever the enemy tries to bring against us—thoughts of fear, lack, and destruction—none of them sticks to us because we are rejoicing.

Second, if we want to walk in restoration, we have to be glad. We have to make a decision to be glad, not sad. The

Bible says that God has made us glad! Knowing Jesus and being assured of His Love and how much He cares for us should be enough to keep our gladness level high.

Third, we are instructed to rejoice. God told us to rejoice and be glad, and when we do that, He's going to give us the former rain and the latter rain together. We're going to have what they had under the old covenant and more besides.

When we do our part and refuse to fear or be moved by the various trials that show up, when we stand firm on the Word of God and lift our hands and lift our voices, rejoicing, then He will give us the former and latter rain together. He will do great things. Our attitude should be, the best is yet to come!

When is He going to do it? When we fear not. When we're glad. When we rejoice! The enemy is trying to terrorize the church. He's trying to terrorize the world. He's trying to get believers to draw back in fear and say, "Oh, bad times are upon us. Bad days are ahead. I'm going to get all I can and can all I get. I'm going to hold on tightly to all that I have. I'm not going to give to the work of God." That is fear, and we're not supposed to operate in fear.

We're living in the time of the latter rain. We're living in the time when Zechariah said, *"Ask the Lord for rain in the time of the latter rain. The Lord will make flashing clouds; He will give them showers of rain"* (Zech. 10:1). But we can't just ask for the rain. We have to "fear not" and we have to be glad and rejoice because our God is pouring out His Spirit.

The time has come for restoration in the Body of Christ. It's time for what verse 24 in Joel chapter 2 talked about— *overflow.* God is into restoring and making things much better than they were before. He is into abundance and overflow.

We're not going to let the devil hold us back. We're going to step into the overflow. We're going to step into restoration.

This wonderful passage of scripture from the Book of Joel goes on to say that God will restore even the years that were eaten by the locust and a bunch of worms. You may have lost years to fear, debt, disease, or worry. But when you start rejoicing, having your full confidence and assurance in the Lord that He is well able to restore the years that the enemy has stolen, that's when the breakthrough will come.

God said that His people would never be ashamed. Don't be ashamed to be known as a believer and to lift your voice in praise and worship unto Him. Our voice is important in releasing joy. Let's read what God says about that in the Book of Jeremiah.

JEREMIAH 33:11

11 "Thus says the LORD: 'Again there shall be heard in this place . . . the voice of joy and the voice of gladness, the voice of the bridegroom and the voice of the bride, the voice of those who will say: "Praise the Lord of hosts, For the Lord is good, For His mercy endures forever"— and of those who will bring the sacrifice ofpraise into the house of the Lord. For I will cause the captives of the land to return as at the first,' says the Lord."

Talk about redemption! Talk about restoration! How does that occur in the midst of a tough situation? By giving a voice to joy.

I like how Jeremiah said that joy brings the sacrifice of praise. Why is it a sacrifice? Because it's offered when things don't look good in the natural. It's a sacrifice for you to lift up your scrawny little hands and say, "Praise the Lord, for his mercy endures forever" when you don't feel like praising the Lord. Power is released when we offer the sacrifice of praise unto the Lord God.

What does giving a voice to joy do for us? I like what the last part of Jeremiah 33:11 says in *The Amplified Bible*: "*For I will cause the captivity of the land to be reversed and return to be as it was at first, says the Lord.*"

Do you want the curse to be reversed in your life? Do you want some things to change? Maybe wrong words have been spoken over you. Maybe there is something destructive in your family that's been passed down from generation to generation. You ought to declare, "It stops now. It's not passing on to me. It's not passing on to my kids. I'm going to rejoice in the Lord my God because He is my Deliverer. He turns my sorrow and mourning into joy, and He reverses the curse."

Whatever was taken from us, rejoicing will get it back and more besides. God wants to bring restoration to His Church and to your individual life. One way that this happens is by giving a voice to joy. As this passage in Jeremiah says, "Joy has a voice." And what is that voice? What is one way that voice is released? Through laughter. Laughter is the voice of joy. In the next chapter, we are going to look in detail at the power of laughter.

CHAPTER 13

He Who Laughs Last

Man is created in the image and likeness of God. According to His Word, we are a spirit; we have a soul, which includes our mind, will, and emotions; and we live in a physical body. God is the One Who created man with these three distinct parts, including our emotions. In other words, He has given us emotions. They are not a bad thing, but they are not to rule over us. When they are yielded to properly, there are benefits in releasing them.

In Ecclesiastes chapter 3, the Bible talks about how there's a time to mourn, a time to weep, a time to live, a time to die, a time to dance, and a time to laugh. Laughter is a good thing. Laughter (a merry heart) is medicine, according to Proverbs 17:22.

As we discussed in the last few chapters, joy is a spiritual force which is expressed and released in various ways. The Bible is full of ways in which joy can be expressed: through praising, singing, shouting, dancing, running, leaping, and yes, laughing! Our Creator, our Father, put a lot of thought into giving us the ability to laugh. He must have put a high premium on our being able to release this emotion.

I read an article about what happens to the muscles in our faces when we laugh. Research on laughter has revealed some very positive physical effects. Under certain conditions, our bodies perform rhythmic, vocalized, and involuntary actions—better known as laughter.[11]

Fifteen facial muscles are used when we laugh. During laughter, there is an electrical stimulation of the zygomatic muscle. [12] (I didn't even know I had one of these, but apparently we all have one.) This is a major muscle in our faces which extends from our cheekbones to the corners of our mouths. It raises the corners of our mouths when we smile. That is just what happens to our *faces* when we laugh, let alone all the other organs of our bodies that are impacted in a positive way.

Laughter is a powerful, God-given force! When we laugh, especially in the face of opposition and difficulty, we are acting like our Father God. Does God laugh? According to the Bible, He certainly does:

PSALM 2:2–4 (Amplified)

2 The kings of the earth take their places; the rulers take counsel together against the Lord and His Anointed One (the Messiah, the Christ). They say,

3 Let us break Their bands [of restraint] asunder and cast Their cords [of control] from us.

4 He Who sits in the heavens laughs; the Lord has them in derision [and in supreme contempt He mocks them].

When God's enemies gather together against Him, what is His response? He's not crying. He's not fretting. He's not saying, "Oh Jesus, oh Holy Ghost. We've got to have a meeting. We need a strategy. We need a plan. The devil has stirred up trouble. Oh my, whatever are We going do?"

No, God doesn't react that way. The verse we just read from the Book of Psalms says that He laughs. Why does He laugh? He's the Alpha. He's the Omega. He's the beginning, the end, and the in-between. And He already knows how it's going to turn out.

He knows that He wins. The Bible says that He holds those in contempt who come against Him and try to stir something up. He's laughing at them. He's mocking them. He's scorning them. He's laughing at the devil. Jesus has already whipped him. Jesus has already spoiled him. Jesus has already made a show of him openly, triumphing over him once and for all!

So, how dumb can the devil be if he is still trying to devise wicked plans? The devil tries to stir up evil dictators and cause trouble in many nations. He tries to get things stirred up all over the earth. That's dumb. It's stupid for him to think that he could ever get the upper hand on God. Jesus has whipped him already. God's Word is established. God's promises are established. God's plans and purposes will stand forever.

That's why the Lord laughs. He cannot be defeated. He always triumphs. And He is never surprised by anything the devil conjures up. Neither is He surprised by anything the devil tries to bring into our lives. Before the attack comes, He has already provided the answer and the way of escape. That is why we can act like Jesus when the devil tries to get us down through his accusations, lies, and attacks.

Just imagine for a moment the enemy having a meeting to discuss how he can bring his accusations against us. He loves to accuse the brethren. Can you picture him trying to come up with all of these plans, various trials, and manifold tests to throw at us?

When that happens, our response should be like the Lord's. We should laugh at the devil and all of his devices because we are confident that Jesus Christ has already given us the victory! We should do what the verse we just read says. *"Let us break* (Satan's) *bands [of restraint] asunder and cast* (his) *cords [of control] from us"* (Ps. 2:3 Amplified).

Any time the enemy tries to bring bondage into our lives we ought to say, "No way. I'm not going to be entangled again with the yoke of bondage. I'm not going back there, devil. You cannot bind me. Whom the Son has set free is free indeed. I've been set free. I'm loosed in the Name of Jesus."

Then we ought to just say, "Ha, ha, ha. . . . You can't touch this, devil. Ha, ha, ha. . . . I'm under the blood. The blood of Jesus protects me. The blood of Jesus cleanses me. The blood of Jesus is able to make me stand. I will not fall. I will not fail. I will not be bound. Ha, ha, ha. . . ." We should rise up and act like the Lord!

You know, the Bible says, *"And God raised us up with Christ and seated us with him in the heavenly realms in Christ Jesus"* (Eph. 2:6 NIV). We're right there beside the Lord. He's raised us up together with Him. When we come up to that place and position that He has provided for us, we ought to act like Him. What is He doing? Remember, Psalm 2:4 says, *"He who sits in the heavens shall laugh."* God is laughing at the devil, because the devil is a defeated foe.

It's time for all of us to come on up! God doesn't want us to be bound. He doesn't want us to live on the lower rungs of life. He doesn't want us to allow the cares, anxieties, and pressures of life to weigh us down.

I know the economy may not look very prosperous in the natural. Things in the world are not always good. But we are not of this world. We live by a different law. We have a higher place, a higher position, and a higher seat. We are seated together in heavenly places with the Lord. We are far above all principalities, powers, might, and dominion (Eph. 1:21).

The devil wants to bring us down. He wants to get us down on his level where we try to deal with him in the natural. But we can't deal with him in the natural. We can't win there. But, thank God, this battle isn't fair! Why? Because we have supernatural weapons. We don't have to deal with the devil in our own ability and strength. We get to do it in the power, might, and ability of God. The weapons of our warfare are not carnal. They're mighty, through God!

We have looked at some of our weapons in previous chapters, but I submit to you that laughter is a primary weapon that you ought to be using against the devil. He wants to fill us with sorrow, mourning, cares, worry, and anxiety. But the Bible says that Jesus has caused sorrow and mourning to flee away from us (Isa. 51:11).

We don't laugh a nervous, anxious laugh. We laugh the laugh of faith, because we know exactly how things are going to turn out. We act on the Word. We draw near to the Lord. We get into His presence. What is in His presence? Psalm 16:11 tells us, *"You will show me the path of life; in Your presence is fullness of joy, at Your right hand there are pleasures forevermore"* (Amplified).

God will show us what? *"The path of life."* He wants to show us the path of life, not the path of death. He wants us to follow the happy road through life. In God, we can have a happy life, a good life.

If you're not happy, if you're not enjoying the journey, then you're on the wrong road. I encourage you to get off that wrong road and step onto the path that God has prepared and prearranged for you.

This verse says there's something else in His presence—fullness of joy. The more you get into His presence, the more full of joy you're going to be. Of course, you tend to act like the people you hang out with. If you're hanging out with sad, sorry, sick people, then you're going to be sad, sorry, and sick yourself.

You may need to get some new friends. You need to hang out with people who are glad. Hang out with people who have the joy of the Lord on the inside. Hang out with people who put a smile on your face and lift you up instead of pulling you down. Don't hang out with people who are bummers, and *don't be a bummer yourself.* Be somebody who is full of joy!

If you're hanging out with Jesus, you'll be a carrier of His life and His joy. The world is sad. The world doesn't have much to rejoice or be happy about. You ought to just walk around smiling and giggling to yourself and make them wonder what you have been up to. People will say, "Why are you so happy? What are you taking? Can I have some of that?" Oh, yes, you certainly can. It's called the joy of the Lord! Be a carrier of His joy wherever you go. God wants our lives to be saturated with His presence, His peace, and His joy.

✴ *God Will Fill Your Mouth With Laughter*

I want to look at some verses in the Book of Job concerning laughter and joy. This may be the last place in the Bible you would think to look if you wanted to find something about joy and laughter. But you can learn some awesome lessons from Job regarding this powerful force. Job 8:20–21 says, *"Behold, as surely as God will never uphold wrongdoers, He will never cast away a blameless man. He will yet fill your mouth with laughter [Job] and your lips with joyful shouting"* (Amplified).

Do you think Job was going through a test? Do you think he had some difficulty? Do you think he faced a bit of a trial? Of course, he did. But do you know what? Those verses we just read say, "God is filling my mouth with laughter." Or we could put it this way: "I'm going to laugh at this situation. I'm going to rejoice in the Lord my God, not because of what's happened, but in spite of it."

Regardless of what's going on around you, no matter how terrible things are, you can still make the choice to rejoice. It's a choice. You can choose to be sad. You can choose to be depressed. Or you can choose to act on the Word of God. You can choose to look down at all that's going wrong or you can choose to look up to where your help comes from. And when you look up, something happens on the inside of you.

If your spirit is looking up and clinging to God and getting into His presence, then all of a sudden, He will fill your mouth with praise. Out of your mouth will come a joyful sound of thanksgiving.

As I shared in a previous chapter, "If Satan can't steal your joy, he can't keep your goods." I know Satan has stolen some things from many people. But we don't have to let him keep them. We can rise up in joy and say, "I'm taking that back in the Name of Jesus. Just as God filled Job's mouth with laughter and brought him restoration from all that was stolen, God is filling my mouth with laughter, and the force of joy is going to bring restoration into my life."

What do you do in difficult situations? How do you act when all hell seems to break loose? I don't live at your house, but I wonder what answer I would get if I were to ask your kids or your mate, "What comes out of their mouths when something goes wrong or they get a bad report or a disturbing phone call?" I'm pretty sure they wouldn't tell me, "Oh, they just start laughing." But if we would act on the Word of God, we would get the results we want!

We can learn a valuable lesson from Job. He was in the heat of a battle, and yet Job 8:21 says, "God is filling my mouth with laughter."

His wife was urging him, "Just curse God and die" (Job 2:9). But he refused to do it. He didn't run from God. He got into God's presence. And what was in God's presence? In His presence was fullness of joy. I can just picture Job getting into the presence of God, and in that presence he began to praise the Lord. And out of his mouth came sounds of laughter.

Let us look at another verse that gives us even more insight into Job's response to destruction and famine:

JOB 5:19–22 (Amplified)

19 He will rescue you in six troubles; in seven nothing that is evil [for you] will touch you.

20 In famine He will redeem you from death, and in war from the power of the sword.

21 You shall be hidden from the scourge of the tongue, neither shall you be afraid of destruction when it comes.

22 At destruction and famine you shall laugh, neither shall you be afraid of the living creatures of the earth.

This passage says that God is going to *"rescue you in six troubles."* That means the trouble is coming from this direction and that direction. It's coming from here, there, and everywhere—from all sides! Perhaps your body is under attack, your car has a flat, you get a note from your kid's teacher, and you get into major strife with your mate. Then your boss puts unreasonable demands on you. Several unexpected bills show up, and finally a seventh thing happens . . . a difficult relative comes to stay with you for a month-long visit!

Even if trouble comes from seven ways, God said He would rescue us. He also promised in verse 20 that He would redeem our lives from death in a time of famine and from the power of the sword during a time of war. And then, in verse 21 He said that He would hide us from the scourge of the tongue and we won't be afraid of destruction when it comes.

What does that remind you of? It reminds me of Psalm 91. We are protected. We are under the shadow of the Most High God. Evil will not come near our dwelling, nor shall any plague come near us. God is our shield. He is our refuge. He is our strength. He is our joy. We don't have to be afraid of destruction, but then He tells us what to do when destruction comes across our path. We have to act on Job 5:22: *"At destruction and famine you shall laugh"* (Amplified).

When was the last time you took that stack of bills that's been staring you in the face, put them on your table, started laughing at them, and declared, "Bills, I call you paid, in the Name of Jesus"? Or when have you pointed to the part of your body that was in pain and said, "Ha, ha, ha. . . . Body, I call you well, in Jesus Name"?

Job 8:21 says, "God will fill my mouth with laughter." And Job knew what to do with the laughter that God filled his mouth with. He laughed at destruction. He laughed at famine. And guess what the result was? It's the same result *you* will get if you act on the Word of God. *"And the Lord turned the captivity of Job and restored his fortunes, when he prayed for his friends; also the Lord gave Job twice as much as he had before"* (Job 42:10 Amplified).

Religion has tried to make Job out to be some kind of martyr or example of false humility. You have probably heard people speaking in their pious voices and saying things like, "I am just like poor old Job. I'm as poor as Job's turkey." But if they really were like Job, they would have received restoration for all that had been stolen from them.

Poor old Job did not end up being poor old Job. God filled his mouth with laughter. He rejoiced in the Lord. He laughed at destruction and famine, and he received back twice as much as he had lost!

The Benefits of Laughter

I think some people are "under-laughed." People can be undernourished, and it's obvious to me that a lot of people are under-laughed! We need to laugh. We need to stop taking life and ourselves so seriously.

There are so many benefits of laughter. Earlier in this chapter we talked about what happens in your face when you laugh. There are also some things that happen in your body.

Some researchers say that healthy people laugh at least fifteen times a day. Three good belly laughs give you optimum benefits. Another study said that a hundred belly laughs equal ten minutes on a rowing machine. Wow, that ought to inspire you! Do you want to get rid of that belly fat? Do some belly laughs. "Ho, ho, ho. . . . Ha, ha, ha. . . ." That ought to do all of us some good.

Now here are some of the therapeutic benefits of laughter that were published in a health journal in 1996. Dr. Lee S. Berk and a fellow researcher, Dr. Stanley Tann, of Loma Linda University in California, have discovered the effects of laughter on the immune system. To date, their published studies have shown that laughter lowers blood pressure. It reduces stress hormones and increases muscle flexibility. It boosts the immune system and raises the levels of infection-fighting T-cells. That sounds good! Laughter also triggers the release of endorphins, the body's natural painkillers.[13] So feel free to take a dose of God's medicine—laughter. Proverbs 17:22 says, *"A merry heart does good, like medicine."*

The world has even discovered the value of laughter. I'm sure we don't want the world to outdo us. We're hooked up with the Inventor of laughter. We ought to be laughing more than anybody else on the face of the earth. We ought to be more full of cheer than anyone else.

I know people go through difficult times and may be faced with depression, and I'm not putting anyone down. But what do they do? They usually go to the doctor and oftentimes he gives them medication.

Now, if you're in that situation, I am not criticizing you. But every time you take a pill, I encourage you to say, "This pill isn't my answer. I'm taking it in faith, but Jesus is my answer. I'm receiving God's medicine." If you're taking a pill for depression, every time you take it, say, "I'm going to take God's medicine for depression—ha, ha, ha! A merry heart does good like a medicine."

People may ask you, "What are you doing?"

Just answer, "Oh, I'm taking my meds. Ha, ha, ha!"

God knew about the importance of laughter before the world knew. But even the world is catching up. I read a newspaper article which said that people were looking for stress relief in "laughter clubs." Isn't that amazing? The world is developing laughter clubs. Not nightclubs—laughter clubs. The article I read talked about how laughter clubs are being started across the nation and around the world. People are gathering to laugh.

Wouldn't it be good if some churches would get the revelation that it's okay to go to church and have some fun? People go to clubs and laugh. But they go to church and sit there as if they're dead. Something is wrong with that. We ought to be laughing in church! We ought to be full of joy because we're full of Jesus.

Don't let the devil steal your joy or your strength! He can't beat a joyful believer and he can't keep what he has stolen. The Bible says in Proverbs 6:31, "*But if he* (the thief) *is found out, he must restore seven times [what he stole]; he must give the whole substance of his house [if necessary—to meet his fine]"* (Amplified).

Don't you want to make the devil pay his just fine for stealing from you? One of his main strategies is to rob us of our joy, so we will cower down in weakness and not rise up and demand that he give back what he has attempted to take from us.

But if we will rejoice and be of good cheer, even in what seems to be a time of famine, the joy we release will attract the restoration we are crying out for! Joy acts like a magnet and draws what we need into manifestation in our lives. It is time to crank up your rejoicing and watch the tide change. You will be amazed at what begins to show up on every wave of joy!

CHAPTER 14

The Great Restorer

The theme of this entire book is restoration. God will restore and make better than before! Our part is to:

1. Forgive and forget.

2. Believe and trust the Lord.

3. Fear not.

4. Pray and praise.

5. Rejoice.

We know God is true to His Word and His character. He is compelled to bring restoration into broken lives. The word *restore* is used numerous times in the Old Testament alone. It comes from the Hebrew word *shuwb* (shoob) and carries the following meanings: to revive or quicken, to turn back, to return, to refresh or repair, to retrieve, to reverse, to put back, and to bring to life.[14]

You may ask, "How does this all become a reality in my life?" Let me emphasize once again that all we need and desire has been provided through the redemptive work of our Lord Jesus Christ. As believers, we can stand in faith on our covenant rights and privileges. The Word of God is full of promises regarding restoration, which we can and should appropriate in our lives.

For example, there are many verses informing us of the awesome news that Jesus bore our sicknesses and diseases which means we don't have to be sick. Among them are Isaiah 53:4–5, Matthew 8:17, and First Peter 2:24. I particularly love the verses that reference healing and restoration together. Here is one from Jeremiah chapter 30—" *'For I will restore health to you And heal you of your wounds,' says the Lord*" (v. 17).

This wonderful scripture not only promises us restoration for our physical bodies, but it also says the Lord will heal our wounds. Of course, this could mean wounds to our physical bodies, such as an injury or broken bone. But I think the writer also wanted us to catch the fact that there is healing available for mental and emotional wounds. God does not want us to suffer with baggage from our past!

We have all had plenty of opportunities to be hurt or severely disappointed by people, and very often those who are close to us. In those cases, the wounds can be especially painful and deep. We may find ourselves needing help to recover. Thank God, the necessary ingredients are found in His presence and His Word!

I like something I heard an older, seasoned minister say, "Can't nobody do me like Jesus!" The world's methods may not have the answer for our recovery, but we can always find a place of refuge and peace in the presence of the Lord.

The following portion of scripture describes perfectly the transformation that happens when we come to the Lord in a time of need. *"God . . . comforts and encourages and refreshes and cheers the depressed and the sinking"* (2 Cor. 7:6 Amplified). Our Heavenly Father is a loving, caring Father who longs to impart encouragement to the discouraged heart. He wants to breathe refreshing into the dry and weary soul, and lift the one who is sinking into the pit of despair!

Most of us are familiar with the 23rd Psalm. Many times we equate that psalm with funerals since it is so often quoted during those services. But it is not just a funeral passage. It is about *restoration*!

PSALM 23:1–3

1 The Lord is my shepherd; I shall not want.

2 He makes me to lie down in green pastures; He leads me beside the still waters.

3 He restores my soul; He leads me in the paths of righteousness For His name's sake.

This passage was such a comfort to me when I was going through a very difficult time in my life. Some things had happened in our ministry that caused me much heartache. There were things being said about me and false accusations being made against me. It was mostly trivial issues, such as someone thinking I was unfriendly or untouchable or wondering why I didn't go to lunch or go shopping with the women in the church.

Keep in mind, this was many years ago when we were first starting out in ministry. I had two small boys at home and a husband who needed lots of love, attention, and support. Honestly, I didn't have the time to go out to lunch just to be social!

If this had happened today, I wouldn't give the rumors or ramblings a second thought. But I was young, and as a young pastor's wife, I wanted to please all the people and make sure everyone liked me and held me in high esteem. If you are a pastor or pastor's wife, I am sure you can relate to the turmoil I was feeling. When we allow other people's opinions to be the deciding factor in determining our peace or happiness, we will be, above all people, most miserable! I finally pressed into the Lord's presence and He brought restoration to my soul and my emotions!

All of us have been hurt or wounded by words, especially those that are untrue and unfounded. We can't allow the words people speak to control us. We control our own destiny! We choose to live in the valley of despair and depression or rise above it.

The Lord began to reveal to me that I was doing exactly what He wanted me to do. In other words, I was pleasing my Heavenly Father. And my husband assured me that I was pleasing him. What more could a girl ask for? On top of that, 99.9 percent of the people in our church were very supportive and loving toward me. Isn't that just like the devil to magnify the 0.1 percent?

If you have gone through a similar situation, let me encourage you to meditate on Psalm 23 and allow our loving Shepherd to restore your soul. Let His rod and staff bring you comfort and safety. Follow Him out of the valley of death and despair right into the path of righteousness and peace!

Restoration: God-Style

All throughout the Word of God, we can find beautiful illustrations of this wonderful principle of restoration. The Book of Ruth depicts a marvelous story of love, loyalty, and commitment and describes the reward for those who possess and operate in these outstanding qualities. Allow expectancy to rise in your heart as you see what God did in this woman's life!

The Bible tells us that there was a great famine in the land of Judah. In order to survive, a man named Elimelech moved his wife, Naomi, and their two sons to the land of Moab. This was most likely a temporary move, their objective being to wait out the famine and then return to their beloved homeland. But tragedy struck unexpectedly when Elimelech died and Naomi was left to support her two sons. She couldn't collect unemployment or live on her husband's fabulous retirement fund. So Naomi and her sons were left to fend for themselves.

We don't know how old her boys were when their father died, maybe still teenagers or young adults. But they had been in Moab long enough to call it home and build relationships with other young people. As life goes, they probably had girlfriends and wouldn't have wanted to leave even if their mother had tried to force them to return to Bethlehem.

So the family stayed in Moab, and the young men both married women from that area. After a ten-year period of time, tragedy struck once again when both of Naomi's sons died. Let's read the first part of this story from the Book of Ruth:

RUTH 1:3–5

3 Then Elimelech, Naomi's husband, died; and she was left, and her two sons.

4 Now they took wives of the women of Moab: the name of the one was Orpah, and the name of the other Ruth. And they dwelt there about ten years.

5 Then both Mahlon and Chilion also died; so the woman survived her two sons and her husband.

What is up with that? Naomi lost her husband and then both of her sons. To quote what some young people might say, "That is messed up!" Naomi could have given up and become bitter toward God. She could have decided to turn her back on Him and forget about keeping His commandments. But that is not what she did!

Naomi was definitely a tenacious woman of God who lived an upright and holy life before her daughters-in-law. And she did it to the degree that when she made the decision to return to Bethlehem, both Ruth and Orpah insisted on going with her. After much persuasion, Orpah returned to her own people. But not Ruth.

RUTH 1:8–14

8 And Naomi said to her two daughters-in-law, "Go, return each to her mother's house. The Lord deal kindly with you, as you have dealt with the dead and with me.

9 The Lord grant that you may find rest, each in the house of her husband." So she kissed them, and they lifted up their voices and wept.

10 And they said to her, "Surely we will return with you to your people."

11 But Naomi said, "Turn back, my daughters; why will you go with me? Are there still sons in my womb, that they may be your husbands?

12 Turn back, my daughters, go—for I am too old to have a husband. If I should say I have hope, if I should have a husband tonight and should also bear sons,

13 would you wait for them till they were grown? Would you

restrain yourselves from having husbands? No, my daughters; for it grieves me very much for your sakes that the hand of the Lord has gone out against me!"

14 Then they lifted up their voices and wept again; and Orpah kissed her mother-in-law, but Ruth clung to her.

Something had happened in Ruth's heart that would not allow her to let Naomi leave without her. I believe it was a work of God that had knit their lives together for a far greater purpose than either one of them could have imagined. Destiny and the very lineage of the people of God were hooked to the choice Ruth made. Thank God, she followed her heart and not the voice of reason. She made the right choice!

Have you ever been in that place where your heart was telling you one thing and your head was screaming something entirely different? From the example that played out in Ruth's life, you can see that it is always advantageous to go with what is in your heart!

The words Ruth spoke to Naomi have been quoted at many a wedding, but they are meant as an example for all of God's people. What commitment! If only all Christians would take this kind of stand!

RUTH 1:16-17

16 But Ruth said: "Entreat me not to leave you, Or to turn back from following after you; For wherever you go, I will go; And wherever you lodge, I will lodge; Your people shall be my people, And your God, my God.

17 Where you die, I will die, And there will I be buried. The Lord do so to me, and more also, If anything but death parts you and me."

Once Naomi and Ruth arrived in Bethlehem, they had to be able to survive. Naomi knew the customs of that day which allowed the poor to pick up any grain that was left by the reapers after each crop was harvested. Since it was now barley harvest, she sent Ruth to glean in the fields. God was leading her every step, and she ended up in the field of a man by the name of Boaz.

Ruth immediately caught his eye, and when he inquired about her and discovered who she was, the Bible says she had favor with him. He instructed Ruth to only glean in his field and told his workers to protect her and make sure they left plenty of grain for her to pick up.

The story got even more interesting when Naomi found out how Ruth's day went! Naomi then gave Ruth a crash course on the customs of marriage in Jewish society. She also explained the responsibility of the nearest kinsman toward the wife of a relative who dies without leaving an heir. If you enjoy a good romance, read the entire Book of Ruth. What a love story!

After Boaz took all the necessary steps according to the law, it was established that he had the right to take Ruth as his wife. Ruth's life was restored. Things immediately turned around for her. The curse was reversed!

She went from sheer poverty—being forced to glean behind the farm workers and dig around in the dirt for a few grains of barley—to become the wife of the *dirt owner!* That was quite a promotion! Only God can do that. But this awesome story doesn't end there.

RUTH 4:13-17

13 So Boaz took Ruth and she became his wife; and when he went in to her, the Lord gave her conception, and she bore a son.

14 Then the women said to Naomi, "Blessed be the Lord, who has not left you this day without a close relative; and may his name be famous in Israel!

15 And may he be to you a restorer of life and a nourisher of your old age; for your daughter-in-law, who loves you, who is better to you than seven sons, has borne him."

16 Then Naomi took the child and laid him on her bosom, and became a nurse to him.

17 Also the neighbor women gave him a name, saying, "There is a son born to Naomi." And they called his name Obed. He is the father of Jesse, the father of David.

Ruth got pregnant on her wedding night. We don't know how long she had been married to Naomi's son, but it was several years, perhaps even ten, and during their entire marriage she had never conceived. She was without children until she made the commitment to go with Naomi to Naomi's homeland and worship Naomi's Living God!

Ruth didn't bring the gods of Moab into Israel. She left them behind and decided to follow the Lord God of Naomi. Didn't she declare, "Your God will be my God"? God so honored her stand that He did exceedingly, abundantly above all she could ask or think. She was not only taken care of, but she now had a caring husband and a son! That is restoration, God-style!

Ruth's son was Obed, the father of Jesse, who was the father of David. Ruth was King David's great-grandmother. What an honor to be in the lineage of David and an even greater honor to be in the lineage of our Lord Jesus Christ!

Not only was this an amazing recovery and restoration for Ruth, but think what it meant to Naomi. The Bible says that as soon as the child was born, the women began to bless the Lord because Naomi now had an heir. It was a shameful thing in those days to be childless or without grandchildren to carry the family name to the next generation. With the birth of Obed, God took away all of Naomi's former grief and shame.

I don't know all that you have been through or what you may be facing at this very moment. But I do know God can and will turn things around for you if you will only lean on His everlasting arms and stand on His eternal promises. Regardless of what you have lost or what may have been stolen from you, if you will only invite the Lord into those areas and release your faith in His goodness, you can enjoy the fullness of His restoration. It may not happen overnight, and it probably won't come without a fight. But the result will be worth whatever it takes!

CHAPTER 15

Pursue and Recover— Double for Your Trouble

As we mentioned in the previous chapter, Ruth and Boaz were the great-grandparents of King David. David's very existence was born out of the restoration God brought to Ruth. And he also experienced major recovery and restoration in his own life!

You're probably familiar with the life of David. He is one of the most esteemed and beloved characters in the Bible. I think it is important to give a summary of some of the highlights in his life, so we can see how powerfully the hand of the Lord moved on his behalf.

David was still a young boy out tending his father's sheep during the reign of King Saul. Saul had been appointed king because the children of Israel insisted on having a physical ruler like all the other nations around them.

Saul was exactly like many people today. He started out obeying and honoring God. But soon he decided he didn't have to live according to God's commands. After several acts of disobedience, the Lord sent the prophet Samuel to inform Saul that the Lord's Spirit had departed from him and his son would not reign after him.

How would you have enjoyed being the bearer of that uplifting message? The Lord took it a step further and told Samuel to go to the house of Jesse and anoint one of his sons to be king in the place of Saul. (See 1 Samuel chapter 16.) Jesse had eight sons, but the Lord did not tell Samuel which one to anoint. Even the prophets of old had to walk by faith!

Jesse had several strong, good-looking sons who seemed to the prophet to be rather "kingly." As one of them passed before Samuel, he even commented that this must be the one—but it wasn't!

Does that bring to mind the saying, "Looks can be deceiving"? Many a man and woman have fallen into a wrong relationship because the person looked "fine." But they soon discovered that "fine" doesn't pay the bills, clean the house, or do the laundry. God wants us to have spouses who are attractive to us. But a relationship can't be built on physical appearance alone.

The Lord made a powerful statement to Samuel: " 'For the Lord does not see as man sees; for man looks at the outward appearance, but the Lord looks at the heart' " (1 Sam. 16:7). All of Jesse's stately sons passed before Samuel, but the Lord did not give him a witness on any of them. Finally, Samuel inquired of Jesse about any remaining sons who were not present.

Of course, David was the youngest and the least likely candidate. He had the job of tending the sheep, and nobody even took the time to inform him of the prophet's visit. After all, he was just a kid. What did it matter if he wasn't present? But that wasn't the Lord's attitude! The Lord knows how to find you, promote you, and reward you!

At the prophet's request, David was summoned. As soon as Samuel laid eyes on him, the Spirit of the Lord informed him that David was the one God had chosen! David was anointed to be the next king of Israel, and the prophet went his way. As far as we know, David went back to tending the sheep. He didn't try to take matters into his own hands and step into the office of king before the time was right.

There is no greater factor in our walk with the Lord than trust. We would all love to have instant manifestations and sudden seasons of reaping and restoration. But it usually doesn't happen that way. David had to walk out his destiny one step at a time, and that is the same way we reach our goals and places of victory.

David was not only a tender of the sheep, but he was also an anointed harp player. King Saul knew his days were numbered as king, but he was having trouble accepting his fate. In First Samuel chapter 16, it says that he was tormented by evil spirits and had a hard time getting any rest or receiving peace. One of Saul's servants suggested they find a great harp player to play for him because music is soothing to the soul. Now, one of the servants had heard David play and knew there was something special about his music. It is called the anointing! David was summoned to the palace and instructed to play for King Saul.

The king was indeed impressed and soothed, not only by David's music, but also by his very presence. He decreed that David would now be his armor bearer. Wherever Saul went, David was there.

On one occasion when David was allowed to return home, he learned that his three older brothers were off in battle with the dreaded Philistines. David's father, Jesse, decided to send him to take his brothers some home-cooked food and see how the Israelites were faring in the war. The scenario that followed is perhaps one of the most famous of all the Bible stories: David versus Goliath.

The Philistine's champion, Goliath, was an enormous giant of a man. He had taunted the Israelites for several days when David arrived at their camp. Goliath was calling for a one-on-one battle between himself and Israel's greatest warrior. But so far, not one solider had stepped up to the plate.

There was something different about David. When he was made aware of the situation, he immediately volunteered for the task! He was met with much opposition from his oldest brother and King Saul. But his faith and confidence in the Lord God of Israel soon persuaded them to let him have a go at this uncircumcised Philistine!

The famous battle is recorded in the Book of First Samuel.

1 SAMUEL 17:45–51

45 Then David said to the Philistine, "You come to me with a sword, with a spear, and with a javelin. But I come to you in the name of the Lord of hosts, the God of the armies of Israel, whom you have defied.

46 This day the Lord will deliver you into my hand, and I will strike you and take your head from you. And this day I will give the carcasses of the camp of the Philistines to the birds of the air and the wild beasts of the earth, that all the earth may know that there is a God in Israel.

47 Then all this assembly shall know that the Lord does not save with sword and spear; for the battle is the Lord's, and He will give you into our hands."

48 So it was, when the Philistine arose and came and drew near to meet David, that David hurried and ran toward the army to meet the Philistine.

49 Then David put his hand in his bag and took out a stone; and he slung it and struck the Philistine in his forehead, so that the stone sank into his forehead, and he fell on his face to the earth.

50 So David prevailed over the Philistine with a sling and a stone, and struck the Philistine and killed him. But there was no sword in the hand of David.

51 Therefore David ran and stood over the Philistine, took his sword and drew it out of its sheath and killed him, and cut off his head with it. And when the Philistines saw that their champion was dead, they fled.

What a phenomenal victory was wrought that day at the hands of a young shepherd boy who trusted in the Lord with all of his heart! There was rejoicing in the camp of the Israelites. Even King Saul was temporarily happy. David was once again at Saul's side and living in the palace with a prestigious position. Here he was serving the very man who he had been told by the prophet that he would replace as king. That had to be an interesting spot!

One day Saul overheard the women singing a song which stirred up jealousy and rage in the core of his being. They were rejoicing and singing these words, " *'Saul has slain his thousands, and David his ten thousands'* " (1 Sam. 18:7). It became obvious to him at that moment that public opinion had changed and the political tide was turning in favor of David. No politician likes to see that happen. What an ego-deflating experience!

I am sure David was very aware of the shift that was occurring, but he did nothing to promote himself by saying or doing anything disparaging against Saul. He remained faithful in his service and continued to honor the king. On the other hand, Saul's behavior became erratic. One minute he was calm, and the next he was throwing a javelin at David while the young man was playing his harp. Talk about being conflicted! Finally David had to flee for his life.

He spent several years running from the madman that Saul had become. I am sure David must have had some moments when he asked, "Why, Lord, why?" and "When, Lord, when?" Those are moments like we've all had in the midst of a season of standing and waiting.

Can you imagine what his thoughts must have been? *Okay, God, what is going on here? I was perfectly happy being a shepherd. I didn't ask for this calling or the anointing to be king. I certainly didn't want to stir up trouble with King Saul. He's crazy! Who would want him trying to kill them? I obeyed You, Lord. I even killed Goliath, and this is the thanks I get! What is going on here?*

Even though David must have had his moments of questioning, the Bible does not record them. All we know is that he remained faithful to God and stayed full of integrity and honor. When he had the opportunity to take Saul's life and end this madness, he refused to do the king any harm. He trusted God to fulfill His promise and allowed Him to bring His plans to pass in his life.

David Inquired of the Lord

There was a really low point in David's life that I want to emphasize and glean valuable truth from in this chapter. During his time of exile, David had acquired an army of devoted followers. They were forced to live in various locations, and at one point they had taken refuge in a place called Ziklag, which was located in the land of the Philistines. The Philistines were at war, so David decided to offer his assistance and bring his army to their aid. As you can imagine, the Philistines did not have precious memories of David, and they vehemently refused his offer!

When David and his men returned to Ziklag, they were not met with a welcoming sight. The city had been burned to the ground and their wives and children taken captive. They were completely devastated and overcome with grief.

Every time I read this story, I'm reminded of what I once heard a minister say about the name *Ziklag*. They said that it literally means "grief." And the city certainly lived up to that name on this particular day!

Up until this point, David's men had remained true and loyal, despite numerous opportunities to quit. But this setback was just too overwhelming for them to handle. There was talk in the ranks of stoning David. *"Now David was greatly distressed, for the people spoke of stoning him, because the soul of all the people was grieved, every man for his sons and his daughters. But David strengthened himself in the Lord his God"* (1 Sam. 30:6).

David didn't know what to do, but he knew where to go and Who to seek. *"So David inquired of the Lord, saying, 'Shall I pursue this troop? Shall I overtake them?' And He answered him, 'Pursue, for you shall surely overtake them and without fail recover all' "* (1 Sam. 30:8).

Pursue and *recover*. Let's look at both of these powerful words in depth. *Pursue* means "to follow in order to catch, to chase, to seek, to achieve or accomplish, to proceed along a course, to engage or keep at an activity."

If you know anything about military procedures, you have probably heard the term, "rules of engagement." There are certain rules, codes, and ethics that soldiers are trained to follow in the time of battle. These are not suggestions. They are not contingent on how the soldier feels. They are commands that must be followed! If they want to achieve their directive and accomplish victory, the rules of engagement must be in place and acted upon. There is a specific course that must be adhered to and not veered from.

In life, there are wounded people who start on the road to recovery and restoration. But then they get sidetracked or distracted and end up off course. There is a price to pay for the restoration we need. We have to be willing to go through the process. Thank God, we don't travel this journey alone! Jesus is with us every step of the way, and His love, mercy, and compassion always lead us into a place of healing and wholeness.

Think about athletes training for the Olympics. Do they just dream of winning the gold medal? Do they just talk and boast of their ability? No! To accomplish their goal, they must actually perform the grueling training, faithfully and consistently, day in and day out, rain or shine, and hot or cold. They must stay the course all the way to the Olympic Games, which are usually years away from the initial day of training.

On the day David received the word *pursue*, he and his men were physically exhausted and emotionally drained. But he knew they must rely on the Lord's strength to carry out His instructions. God never places a task before us which He won't provide the wisdom, ability, and strength for us to accomplish.

God didn't give David the whole picture or all the details of how the recovery was going to occur. But He did give David enough information to help him step out in faith and expectancy. God said, "Without fail, you will recover all!"

The word *recover* is very similar in meaning to *restore*, but it carries a slightly different connotation. *Recover* means "to get back, to regain, to regain control, such as in a favorable judgment in a lawsuit."

As believers we could interpret *recover* in this fashion. The devil may attempt to kill, steal, and destroy, but in the corridors of Heaven there has been a judgment against him. All the control he desired has been regained by our Lord Jesus Christ. *Jesus won every case for us!* It is settled through His redemptive work. We have, can, and must recover all. The written law of the Word of the Living God has ruled in our favor—"Pursue and recover all!"

That is a powerful word, and as David acted upon it, the recovery happened just as the Lord had promised him! "*So David recovered all that the Amalekites had carried away, and David rescued his two wives. And nothing of theirs was lacking, either small or great, sons or daughters, spoil or anything which they had taken from them; David recovered all*" (1 Sam. 30:18–19). How powerful is that? There was nothing missing which had been stolen from them. Everything was returned to David and his men. They recovered all!

Don't you love happy endings? But that wasn't the end of the story. God wasn't finished being God and showing Himself strong on David's behalf. *"Also David captured all the flocks and herds [which the enemy had], and the people drove those animals before him and said, This is David's spoil"* (1 Sam. 30:20 Amplified).

Notice the word *also*. God is into the "also!" The word *also* simply means "in addition" or "more added to." For example, I might tell you that my husband ate a hot dog at the ballpark and then say, "He *also* had nachos, popcorn, pizza, and ice cream." The hot dog was just the beginning of much more to come!

David and his men must have been thrilled to get their wives, children, and all of their possessions back. But God did something that was above and beyond merely recovering what had been lost. He added to them! The spoils from the enemy were the reward for the trouble and anguish they had gone through. Not only that, but this was a turning point in David's life. It wasn't long after this incident that King Saul and his son Jonathan were killed in battle, and David rose up to be king. God's word from many years earlier finally came to pass!

Keep Hope Alive!

I believe one thing David never lost was hope. If we are going to enjoy all God has planned for our lives and see our dreams come to pass, we must keep hope alive! In Psalm 42, David was obviously going through a rough season, but even in his anguish, he repeatedly used the phrase, *Hope in God.* Talk about positive self-talk! His emotions and feelings were pulling him in one direction, yet he reminded himself to have *hope in God.*

Our hope, faith, and trust can't be in a person, position, or possessions. Only God is worthy or capable of handling that place. Misplaced faith or hope will only lead to major disappointment and disillusionment. *"Hope deferred makes the heart sick, but when the desire is fulfilled, it is a tree of life"* (Prov. 13:12 Amplified).

If we lose hope, our hearts will be heavy, and we can even become open prey to sickness and disease. Being down on the inside will affect our countenance and our bodies. We are not created to live without hope! We must believe the "God of all hope" will revive and renew our hope, so that we will be able to comprehend the awesome plans and future He has in store for us. *"May the God of your hope so fill you with all joy and peace in believing [through the experience of your faith] that by the power of the Holy Spirit you may abound and be overflowing (bubbling over) with hope"* (Rom. 15:13 Amplified).

When a container is bubbling over with a liquid or substance, it means there is so much the container can't hold it all. It is flowing over the top and running down the sides! Our hope "meter" is supposed to register *overflow*, not be so low that it doesn't even register.

There is a beautiful verse in the Book of Zechariah concerning hope: *"Return to the stronghold [of security and prosperity], you prisoners of hope; even today do I declare that I will restore double your former prosperity to you*" (Zech. 9:12 Amplified). If you are going to be a prisoner of something, it might as well be hope. We should be locked in to the promises of the Word of God, tied up in His love, and guarded by His peace!

Make Jesus your stronghold and security. He has promised to restore double all that has been stolen. That should cause our hope, faith, and joy to rise to a new level!

I heard a minister once use the phrase "double for your trouble," and it is forever branded in my heart! I am not sure if David received double immediately after the Ziklag incident. But if you look at the rest of his life, it was apparent that *he was abundantly blessed*!

Consider this passage of scripture: *"For your shame ye shall have double; and for confusion they shall rejoice in their portion: therefore in their land they shall possess the double: everlasting joy shall be unto them"* (Isa. 61:7 KJV).

Oftentimes, shame is associated with loss, especially if the loss has to do with a broken relationship, such as an ugly, painful divorce. A few years ago, I was speaking on the subject of restoration at a women's conference. As I read this verse, the Lord seemed to want me to emphasize how He could restore what had been lost or forfeited due to a failed marriage.

Out of my own mouth, I heard the words, "The Lord will give you double for your trouble. No, not two husbands, but one who treats you *twice as good*!" This was quite a revelation for some women at that meeting who were believing for godly mates.

Maybe you are in that same position right now. It is not impossible or too difficult for God to bring the right person into your life, at just the right time! Don't settle for anything other than God's very best. You are worth His best, and the right person is worth the wait.

The passage of scripture we just read in Isaiah 61 also says, *"for confusion they shall rejoice."* God is not the author of confusion, so if you are full of wavering and unsettled in your heart about a relationship or decision, take time to hear from God and allow peace to establish your ways. When there is peace instead of confusion, there will also be joy!

Let's look at Isaiah 61:7 in *The Amplified Bible*—*"Instead of your [former] shame you shall have a twofold recompense; instead of dishonor and reproach [your people] shall rejoice in their portion. Therefore in their land they shall possess double [what they had forfeited]; everlasting joy shall be theirs."*

What does it mean to receive recompense? One definition of *recompense* is "amends made, as for damage or loss." Perhaps the company you work for provides Workers' Compensation for its employees. This benefit is in place to compensate you if you are injured or hurt on the job and unable to perform your regular responsibilities.

If companies will do that for their employees, how much more will your Heavenly Father provide for you and compensate you when you have been hurt or injured by life? His Workers' Compensation plan is out of this world! He doesn't just give us barely enough to survive. He offers us soundness, wholeness, and restoration in every area of our lives. Let Him touch you with the healing and restoring touch you so desperately desire!

I love the words to the old song, "He Touched Me," by William Gaither.

Shackled by a heavy burden,
'Neath a load of guilt and shame.
Then the hand of Jesus touched me,
And now I am no longer the same.

He touched me, oh He touched me.
And oh the joy that floods my soul.
Something happened and now I know
He touched me, and made me whole![15]

God wants to remove any shame, dishonor, or reproach from our lives and replace them with His peace and joy! He has promised us restoration and everlasting joy. As I've said before, joy is a necessary ingredient for receiving the manifestation of complete restoration.

Don't allow your joy to be stolen or zapped out of your life through difficulties and hardships. If you are a born-again Christian, you have a joy that compares with nothing else in the world. If you are not yet a Christian or follower of Christ, you can be if you pray the simple prayer at the close of this book.

Let me refer once again to the life of King David. In Psalm 51:12, he penned the phrase, *"Restore to me the joy of Your salvation."* There are too many Christians who have lost the joy they once had in being a child of the Most High God—part of the redeemed and blood-bought Church!

On our worst day, we should still be able to look up and declare, "I am on my way to Heaven, even if it feels like I'm going through hell. God is for me, He is in me, and He is with me. He is turning this mess into a message!" If you sense the joy you once enjoyed has been drained from your life, boldly join David in a prayer requesting God to restore the joy of your salvation.

When you begin to realize all that God has done, is doing, and will do for you, that temporary meltdown will melt down in size! Picture a snowball trying to survive in the hot, July sunshine. It is no match for the heat and force of the sun.

You and I have the light of the Son of God available to us. No sickness, no financial setback, no relationship difficulty, or anything else we may face will be able to withstand the brightness of the "Son of Righteousness"! His glorious light will always dispel and override any darkness. There is nothing that can compare to the power, might, and ability of our God! Remember, He can and He will restore and make better than before, and He is a Master at fixing any disaster!

Salvation Prayer

Dear Heavenly Father,

I come to You in the Name of Jesus.

Your Word says, *"the one who comes to me I will by no means cast out"* (John 6:37), so I know You won't cast me out, but You take me in and I thank You for it.

You said in Your Word, *" 'Whoever calls on the name of the Lord shall be saved' "* (Rom. 10:13). I am calling on Your Name, so I know You have saved me now.

You also said, *"If you confess with your mouth the Lord Jesus and believe in your heart that God has raised Him from the dead, you will be saved. For with the heart one believes unto righteousness, and with the mouth confession is made unto salvation"* (Rom. 10:9–10). I believe in my heart Jesus Christ is the Son of God. I believe that He was raised from the dead for my justification, and I confess Him now as my Lord.

Because Your Word says, *"with the heart man believes unto righteousness"* and I do believe with my heart, I have now become the righteousness of God in Christ (2 Cor. 5:21) . . . And I am saved!

Thank You, Lord!

Notes

1 For the complete account of this story, please see the minibook *Don't Blame God* by Kenneth E. Hagin, available through Faith Library Publications.

2 John H. Sammis, 1887. "Trust and Obey." Public Domain.

3 persevere.Thesaurus.com. *Roget's 21st Century Thesaurus, Third Edition.* Philip Lief Group 2009. http://www.thesaurus.com/browse/persevere.

4 *New Spirit-Filled Life® Bible,* copyright © 2002 by Thomas Nelson, Inc.

5 Webster's II New Riverside University Dictionary. (Boston: The Riverside Publishing Company, 1984), 702.

6 R. Kelso Carter, 1886. "Standing on the Promises." Public Domain.

7 David B. Guralnik, ed., Webster's New World Dictionary, 2nd college ed. (Cleveland: William Collins & World Publishing, 1974), 41.

8 always.Dictionary.com. *The American Heritage® Dictionary of the English Language, Fourth Edition.* Houghton Mifflin Company, 2004. http://dictionary.reference.com/browse/always.

9 Jerry Savelle, *If Satan Can't Steal Your Joy . . . He Can't Keep Your Goods* (Tulsa: Harrison House, Inc., 2002).

10 Strong's Hebrew Dictionary, #1523 *guwl.*

11 Marshall Brain. "How Laughter Works." 01 April 2000. HowStuff Works.com. http://health.howstuffworks.com/human-nature/emotions/other/laughter1.htm.

12 2010 Encyclopedia Britannica Online (function in facial expressions (*in* humour (human behaviour)). http://www.britannica.com/EBchecked/topic/276309/humour

13 Lee S. Berk, "The Laughter-Immune Connection: New Discoveries" *Humor and Health Journal* 5:5 (September/October 1996): 1–5.

14 Strong's Hebrew Dictionary, #7725 *shuwb.*

15 William J. Gaither, "He Touched Me" © 1963 William J. Gaither.

Why should you consider attending

RHEMA
Bible Training Center?

Here are a few good reasons:

- Training at one of the top Spirit-filled Bible schools anywhere

- Teaching based on steadfast faith in God's Word

- Growth in your spiritual walk coupled with practical training in effective ministry

- Specialization in the area of your choosing: Youth or Children's Ministry, Evangelism, Pastoral Care, Missions, Biblical Studies, or Supportive Ministry

- Optional intensive third-year programs: School of Worship, School of Pastoral Ministry, School of World Missions, and General Extended Studies

- Worldwide ministry opportunities—while you're in school

- An established network of churches and ministries around the world who depend on RHEMA to supply full-time staff and support ministers

- A two-year evening school taught entirely in Spanish is also available. Log on to **www.cebrhema.org** for more information.

Call today for information or application material.
1-888-28-FAITH (1-888-283-2484)
www.rbtc.org

RHEMA Bible Training Center admits students of any race, color, or ethnic origin.

OFFER CODE—BKORD:PRMDRBTC